W9-DEE-036

WITHDRAWN

Eliot's Compound Ghost

Eliot's Compound Ghost

Influence and Confluence

Leonard Unger

The Pennsylvania State University Press
University Park and London

for Sherley

Library of Congress Cataloging in Publication Data
Unger, Leonard.
  Eliot's compound ghost.

  Includes index.
    1. Eliot, T. S. (Thomas Stearns), 1888–1965—
Knowledge—Literature. I. Title.
PS3509.L43Z8819   821'.912   81–47173
ISBN 0–271–00292–1   AACR2

Designed by Dolly Carr

Printed in the United States of America

Contents

Acknowledgments

Because I know where to begin but not where to end, I will name only a few of the persons to whom I owe thanks for the various kinds of help I received in writing this book and in bringing it to publication. At all stages of its production, Professor Peter Firchow was unfailing in his concerned interest and as a wise and candid critic. Others who sustained me as gracious audience to my spoken and written words are Professors Thomas Clayton, Norman Fruman, Michael Hancher, Balachandra Rajan, and my former students Teresa Ebert and Elise Howell Scherer. If it were not for Professor Stanley Weintraub's effective initiative and interest, I might not have had this occasion for acknowledging my debt to him and others. I want to thank Professors Armin Paul Frank and Grover Smith for their essential support and valuable suggestions, and especially for advice regarding the Introduction. For his confidence, patience and advice, I am grateful to Mr. John M. Pickering, Editorial Director of The Pennsylvania State University Press. My wife, to whom the book is dedicated, deserves thanks beyond what I will try to say here. Wherever the book may fall short of any standards, only I am responsible.

Parts of this book were written while I was on sabbatical leave from the University of Minnesota and during a period of residence at Yaddo, so I am pleased to express my gratitude for the privileges and advantages which I enjoyed.

I
Introduction:
The Purpose of Recognition

These things have served their purpose: let them be.
Little Gidding

"I can name positively certain poets whose work has influenced me. I can name others whose work, I am sure has not; there may still be others of whose influence I am unaware, but whose influence I might be brought to acknowledge; but about Poe I shall never be sure." This statement, made by T. S. Eliot in 1948,[1] provides four categories on the subject of literary influence, which is largely the subject of this book. The statement provides the broad features of an outline that could be developed in greater detail. In fact, some excellent outlines and systematic discussions of this subject already exist.[2] But generalizations can become inadequate and inappropriate when applied to or abstracted from particular cases. Furthermore, one person's analysis of the subject into a scheme of categories may differ from another's. For example, Eliot's statement is itself a category in the respect that it is the poet's own point of view as distinguished from a reader's. More specifically, Eliot does "name positively" as a substantial influence on his early work "in 1908 or 1909 ... the later Elizabethan drama."[3] Yet it has long been my opinion (and I recall that of others to the same effect) that no such influence is discernible in the poems of *Prufrock and Other Observations*. A different but also comparable point is made in one critic's statement, as follows: "It is a moot question how much of the unmistakable Browningesque element in T. S. Eliot's technique is traceable (despite his own disclaimer) to his reading of Browning's poetry itself and how much to his acknowledged indebtedness to Ezra Pound, whose early work, in turn, as Pound has often said, was deeply influenced by Browning. A third possibility, which does not exclude the other two, is that Eliot's use of the dramatic monologue and of colloquial diction is simply one evidence of the influence Browning had upon poetic technique in general during the first decades of the twentieth century."[4] This comment indicates how elusive, complicated, and indeterminate the question of influence may be, both for the critic and the poet. If Browning was an influence and Eliot disclaimed it, we can only speculate as to why he did so. He may have preferred to disclaim it because he considered it minimal and because he had a low opinion of or antipathy toward Browning. Possibly for the same reason (or some other?) he may have suppressed an awareness, actually disclaiming the influence, so that we must describe such influence as irreversibly unconscious. Possibly, also, dramatic monologue and colloquial diction were already so general (as the critic declares they were) that Eliot felt no measure of debt, direct or indirect, to Browning. Furthermore, dramatic monologue and colloquial diction are prominent in the poetry of Laforgue, who is unquestionably the most conspicuous influence in Eliot's early work and whom Eliot names as the first major influence along with later Elizabethan drama. This leads to the consideration that it is the critic himself who has been influenced by Browning, having experienced a forceful association between the two poets, specifically their dramatic monologues. Some readers, including myself, would not use so strong a term as "unmistakable"—I would prefer "discernible." The suffix (-esque) of the eponymous adjective softens some of the force of "unmistakable." If there is no other way of making Browning's name adjectival, some other locution might have been used, such as "Browning element," "element of Browning," or "influence of Browning." As for later Elizabethan drama, while none of its features are to be found in Eliot's early work (as they are in "Gerontion" and The Waste Land), it is still possible that he felt indebted in some ways (for stimulation and motivation) to his reading of that literature. It is also possible that he wished to attenuate the uniquely conspicuous debt to Laforgue of the early poems and his own acute awareness of that debt.

I have been moving among several views of a particular question of influence: my own, another reader's and that of the poet. Another example of the fact that influence and the degree of influence may be indeterminable is Eliot's statement, "about Poe I shall never be sure." This can be interpreted as evidence that Eliot had at least faint intimations of influence by Poe but that he could not (or would not) specify its nature. Critics have occasionally related Eliot's practice with Poe's dictum that no poem should be longer than what can be read at a single sitting, but no one to my knowledge has defined or located a specific feature of influence. Hugh Kenner stated that "Gerontion was written by an American, who...resembles no other American writer so much as he does Poe."[5] Kenner meant by this that as Americans these poets, because detached from English traditions, were more acutely aware of the traditions (than native Englishmen) and used them more deliberately—but each in accordance with his own principles of selection. Striking as the resemblance may be (according to Kenner), it is not proof, or even claim, of an influence. Matthiessen had earlier made a similar point, observing that Eliot shared with earlier American writers (naming Poe, as well as Thoreau, Hawthorne, Dickinson, and Henry James) "the conditions of American life, ... isolation of the individual from the centre of European culture."[6] It is true, of course, that Eliot was avowedly influenced by some of the *Symboliste* poets of France, and that these poets were avowedly influenced by Poe, so that it may be said there was an *indirect* influence by the earlier on the later American. Eliot could have made the carefully ambivalent statement on his relation with Poe because he was so well aware of these French connections, and because there might have been a direct influence of Poe somehow combined with the indirect influence transmitted (and transmuted) by the French poets.

The cases of Browning and Poe as possible influences on Eliot are examples of how conjectural and problematic is the subject of influence. This view of the subject has long prevailed and was well expressed by André Morize in 1922: "Influence by its very nature does not always declare itself by precise and well-defined signs; its study does not admit of the same exactness as, for instance, the investigation of sources. Frequently, it consists in following the capricious, unexpected meanderings of a stream whose waters are led hither and thither by the accidental contour of the ground and take their color from the various tributaries and the soil through which they flow—at times even disappearing for a space, to reappear farther on."[7] The distinction here between influence and source can be qualified by the fact that some influences are indeed declared "by precise and well-defined signs," by the evidence of sources, although there are many cases where a determinable or conspicuous source is no more than that, a single allusion, echo, or borrowing. Even some claims of source on the basis of "precise and well-defined signs" may be questionable or inadmissible. One such case, in my view, is Harry Blamires' offering of Longfellow's *Hiawatha* as an influence and a source of echoes in *Four Quartets*, especially in *Burnt Norton* and *Little Gidding*: "Though the 'longest river' of *LG* 246 is the river of time, of human history (as in *The Dry Salvages*), it is no doubt more especially associated with the Mississippi, the world's longest river, whose source is in the state of Minnesota. Here again then, 'at the source of the longest river' (*LG* 246), we are in the territory of the Dacotahs, and it is impossible not to hear the voice of Minnehaha in 'the voice of the hidden waterfall' (LG 247), calling to the youthful Hiawatha on his journey to fetch his bride. (Longfellow's own note on 'Minnehaha' puts the matter beyond dispute: 'Laughing Water; a waterfall on a stream running into the Mississippi between Fort Snelling and the Falls of St. Antony.')"[8] Blamires' recurring attention to this subject may help us understand how he became persuaded that "it is impossible not to hear" voices from Hiawatha in Four Quartets and why he regards the matter as "beyond dispute," but the positiveness with which he makes his claim may not persuade other readers—as I am not persuaded. The "strong brown god" river of The Dry Salvages and "the longest river" of Little Gidding, whatever else they are, are also and certainly the Mississippi River, and Minnehaha Falls is one of that river's tributaries, but these facts do not lead to the conclusion that Longfellow's poem was both source and influence in Eliot's poem. If at some time it should be revealed that Eliot had acknowledged (e.g., in notes or a letter) the relation with Hiawatha, then I should be both surprised and persuaded. In his Introduction to an edition of Mark Twain's Huckleberry Finn[9] Eliot made it implicitly clear, with literal and conceptual details, that he associated Huck Finn's Mississippi River with the river of his own poem. And he said elsewhere, "For Twain's readers anywhere, the Mississippi is the river."[10] Another relevant case is that of Kipling's story "They," reported by Helen Gardner as a possible source of the children and garden imagery of Burnt Norton.[11] I was originally unimpressed by this suggestion, so that when Elisabeth Schneider offered Oscar Wilde's fairy tale "The Selfish Giant" as a more likely and more substantial source than Kipling's story,[12] I readily agreed. But it turns out that Gardner has the last word so far, documented by Eliot's letter to John Hayward (5 August 1941) where Eliot states that he recognized the debt to Kipling while re-reading the story five years after composing his poem.[13] (See Chapter VII below for a fuller account of Kipling's and Wilde's stories.) Of course, Blamires, Gardner, and Schneider, like all students of Eliot's poetry, have undoubtedly been aware that many sources flow into Eliot's imagery of children in the garden.

The stories of Kipling and Wilde may very well be sources of Eliot's imagery and the ideas conveyed by it, but this does not mean that the stories, or their authors, have been an influence. Even this view, clear and simple as it is on one level, needs qualification, for the questions of source and influence, and the relation between them in specific cases, are complex and multi-faceted, especially in the poetry of Eliot. The qualification I have in mind involves the fact that the children-garden imagery is a recurring motif and one of the centers of greatest intensity in Eliot's poetry and plays. Because this imagery abounds with echoes from many sources—the biblical Garden of Eden, Milton's *Paradise Lost*, Dante's *Vita Nuova* and *Divine Comedy*, Carroll's *Alice in Wonderland*, D. H. Lawrence's story "The Shadow in the Rose Garden," and more, including Kipling and Wilde—the entire body or collectivity of sources does constitute an influence. Some of these participate in that influence, but they are otherwise merely sources. An early and oft-quoted statement of Eliot's is relevant here: "The poet's mind is in fact a receptacle for seizing and storing up numberless feelings, phrases, images, which remain there until all the particles which can unite to form a new compound are present together."[14] Eliot's own poetry, before and after the time of this statement, is (to understate the case) a striking illustration of this principle. But the statement is too general and too impersonal to serve as a wholly appropriate account. It is not enough to say that Eliot's children-garden imagery is a compound of "particles which can unite." What we have in this case and in others is a dynamics of correspondence by which a variety of sources becomes both a confluence and an influence. Where such confluence exists, it is the poet himself who figures in the equation of influence: if a number of sources converge on the poetry, it is also true that the sources have been drawn into the poetry by the poet's experience (at whatever levels of consciousness) of association. Eliot tells us as much within the poetry: "Other echoes/ Inhabit the garden. Shall we follow?" (*Burnt Norton* I). One of the meanings is that the poetry derives from and leads to its sources— although readers may not be in total accord as to where the echoes lead—as in the case of *Hiawatha*.

Mentioning that (once) famous poem again calls to mind an example of how complicated and problematic are the subjects of source and influence. Eliot's poem "Marina" has positively for its source Shakespeare's play *Pericles, Prince of Tyre* and is one of many manifest instances of Shakespeare's influence on Eliot's poetry. The following passage from "Marina" contains the children-garden motif:

> Whispers and small laughter between leaves and hurrying feet
> Under sleep, where all the waters meet.

While we might allow that this passage shares all the sources claimed for the motif in general, we might not include Shakespeare's play among those sources. *Pericles* is rather the source of a poem which in turn is the context of a source-rich motif. The *Hiawatha* relevance is of course in the words "laughter" and "where all the waters meet," which alert us to Longfellow's note on "Laughing Water" and the Mississippi River. Curiously, Blamires fails to take notice of this passage in any of his many references to *Hiawatha,* nor is "Marina" even mentioned in his book. On this score and on the matter of *Hiawatha* Blamires is an example of the fact that all of us can and do commit errors of recognition, on the one hand making questionable claims out of strictly subjective associations, and on the other failing to notice particulars that are relevant to our purposes. This frailty of scholars and critics is one of the subjects of this book. If what I have called "errors of recognition" proceed from such frailty, they also proceed from what is inevitable and valuable in our experience of reading literature—that is, responding with associations that come from our own experience, including the experience of reading. For an example, I am reminded of Robert Frost's fine little poem "A Patch of Old Snow," where the dirty remnant of snow is compared to a piece of old newspaper—and the poem ends with the statement, "The news of a day I've forgotten, /If I ever read it." For me Frost's poem includes a facet of meaning which is a wry comment on François Villon's famous refrain, *"Où sont les neiges d'antan?"* ["Where are the snows of yesteryear?"] Villon is thus a presence in (or behind) Frost's poem, as I have come to read it—yet possibly not an acceptable presence for other readers.

The following chapters offer some new sources for Eliot's poetry and new influences—evidence that certain influences were more extensive and more intense than had previously been recognized. The accumulation of evidence leads, moreover, to the observation (as stated above) that the relation among the influences is relevant to Eliot's development as a poet and to the continuity and interrelatedness of the poems. This view can be partially illustrated here by considering (primarily) some of the poems of *Prufrock and Other Observations.* The singularly conspicuous influence at this opening state of Eliot's career as a poet is, of course, Jules Laforgue. Of these poems the earliest, "Conversation Galante" (written in 1909), is actually modeled on Laforgue's "Autre Complainte de Lord Pierrot." Eliot had first read the poem during the eventful experience of discovering Laforgue in Arthur Symons' *The Symbolist Movement in Literature,* where it is quoted in full. Eliot's poem is so close to Laforgue's that it is on the border of being a free translation. It is certainly an adaptation. If other poems of Eliot's were as closely modeled on the works of other writers, F. W. Bateson's repeated charge of plagiarism would be justified. But "Conversation Galante" may be regarded as redeemed from plagiarism by the fact that it has a meaningful place in Eliot's development and in the continuity of Eliot's poems. The poem is a miniature dramatization of the human condition seen as the inescapable isolation of each person—to be expressed in *The Waste Land* as "each in his prison/Thinking of the key, each confirms a prison." Like Laforgue's poem, Eliot's is a dialogue between a man and a woman, as reported by the man, in which the speakers fail to communicate. Eliot produces a heavier irony than Laforgue in calling the dialogue a "conversation" whereas Laforgue's poem is a "complainte." In both poems the woman is subjected to the man's irony, for the man is ironically aware that no communication occurs. Both poems end with similar words, but also with a difference: whereas "*C'était donc sérieux?*" is the man's remark, it is the woman who concludes with "Are we then so serious?" With the difference in title and conclusion, Eliot has added a weight of irony beyond that of his model.

"Portrait of a Lady" and "The Love Song of J. Alfred Prufrock," completed in 1910 and 1911 respectively and Laforguean in various aspects of style, are decidedly Eliot's own poems. Yet these show a significant continuity from "Conversation Galante." "Portrait of a Lady" is an ironical title in that it is the man who is more vividly and more significantly portrayed. Like the earlier poem, this too is an account of failed conversation and unachieved relation, as reported by the man. Here too the woman is subjected to the man's irony, but the man is subjected to the poet's irony, and to his own as well. As for "Prufrock," that title is ironical in its own terms, and also in relation to the poem. In this poem there are fragments of conversation, of imagined conversation and of failed conversation—"That is not what I meant, at all"—but for the most part the conversation is between the man and himself, an "interior monologue," as the poem has frequently been described. There is some irony at the expense of women: "In the room the women come and go/Talking of Michelangelo." The plural makes the female even more remote than in the other poems. Similarly remote is the impersonal "one": "If one, settling a pillow by her head," and "If one, settling a pillow or throwing off a shawl...." In the title, Prufrock is subjected to the poet's irony, and in the poem it is self-irony and self-mockery which prevail. Prufrock is more vividly isolated and more preoccupied with his isolation than are the men of "Portrait of a Lady" and "Conversation Galante."

"The greatest debts are not always the most evident; at least, there are different kinds of debt."[15] Eliot made this statement in 1950 at the opening of a paragraph in which he compares and contrasts his debt to Laforgue and his debt to Dante, both of them great debts. His meaning surely is that in the poems of *Prufrock* the former is "most evident" and the latter not so. In the same essay, with reference to Dante, he made a similar statement: "The important debt does not occur in relation to the number of places to which a critic can point a finger...."[16] In speaking, here and elsewhere, of the debt to Dante, Eliot meant a debt that continued throughout all stages of his career—and that began at the earliest stage. This early influence of Dante was affirmed when in 1961 he again spoke in close conjunction of the debts to Laforgue and Dante, saying in one paragraph that it is Laforgue "to whom I owe more than to any one poet in any language," and in the next paragraph making this statement: "There is one poet...who impressed me profoundly when I was twenty-two....the poet I speak of is Dante....Dante's astonishing economy and directness of language—his arrow that goes unerringly to the centre of the target...."[17] Eliot was twenty-two in 1910, the year in which he composed "Portrait of a Lady" and much of "The Love Song of J. Alfred Prufrock."

While no critic has pointed a finger to places in the poetry of *Prufrock* where there is a debt to Dante, some have found connections on that score. One critic has made the following comment: "Dante's *Divine Comedy* familiarizes its reader with the path by which the earliest intimations of immortality and felicity in childhood love become transmuted to the boundless felicity of the highest love....As in Dante's masterpiece, the experience of that path is the central theme of Eliot's poetry from *The Love Song of J. Alfred Prufrock* to the end of *Four Quartets*."[18] Other critics have come close to pointing a finger in comments on the epigraph—Guido da Montefeltro's words to Dante, *Inferno* xxvii, 61–6—placed by Eliot at the opening of "Prufrock." One of these critics has said: "The epigraph to the poem expands the context of Prufrock's frustration....He, like Guido, is in hell...."[19] Another critic made much the same point with the comment, "From these Italian words the English speech moves forward without a break," and he observed that Prufrock is in a kind of hell, "a hell neither sustained by theology nor gradated by degrees of crime...."[20] But there is another connection between Eliot's poetry and this epigraph, which I quote in translation: "If I thought my answer were to one who ever could return to the world, this flame should shake no more; but since none ever did return alive from this depth, if what I hear is true, without fear of infamy I answer thee."[21] The connection between Guido and Prufrock, besides the state of hell in which each exists, is the dramatic irony to which each is subject. For Guido the irony is that Dante did return to the world to report the sinner's infamy—which was the impossible attempt, in Guido's words, "to repent and will a thing at the same time."[22] For Prufrock a comparable irony is in lamenting an isolation which at the same time he cherishes. This feature of contradiction, or contrast, is broadly emphasized by the absurdity of the title of the poem and by the relation between the title and the poem itself, for Prufrock's monologue is in no sense a love song—unless the revelation of melancholy self-love could be so called. If Prufrock is self-mocking, he is also self-regarding. He could appropriately say, with the young man of "Portrait of a Lady," "I remain self-possessed," for one of the meanings of this expression is definitely, and ironically, narcissistic. The relevance of the epigraph from Dante to the poetry of *Prufrock and Other Observations* resides then in effects of irony and interior conflict, effects which even more conspicuously are similar to those of Laforgue.

More evident than the influence of Dante on Eliot's early poems has been that of Henry James. F. O. Matthiessen, both in his book on Eliot and in *American Renaissance,* repeatedly referred to the Jamesian qualities in Eliot's writing, including the early poems, as in this comment: "The more one thinks of Eliot in relation to James, the more one realizes the extent of the similarities between them. . . . Prufrock's rankling inability to give himself to life and the kind of frustration embodied in Eliot's 'Portrait of a Lady' find their parallels many times in James."[23] Comparable observations have been made by other critics, including myself.[24] Grover Smith found in these poems "a psychological method that one might ascribe to a close study of Henry James, a study which could have affected, as strongly as imitation of Laforgue, the dramatic organization of Eliot's verse."[25] Another critic declared that "It is a quintessentially Jamesian experience which lies at the heart of his work. The tragedy is that of one who can perceive but cannot act, who can understand and remember but cannot communicate."[26] It has often been noted that Eliot used a title identical with that of James's late novel, *Portrait of a Lady.* Some of the specific "parallels . . . in James" that have been noted are Lambert Strether of *The Ambassadors* and the male protagonists of "Crapy Cornelia," "The Beast in the Jungle," and *The Aspern Papers,* each of whom declines a proffered relationship with a woman, and in each case there is a facet of irony. "The Beast in the Jungle" tells of a man who becomes shatteringly aware of a woman's abiding love for him only after she has died. The narrator of *The Aspern Papers* is a scholar who is passionately eager to obtain possession of love-letters written to Juliana Bordereau by the (fictional) early nineteenth-century Byron-like poet Jeffrey Aspern, so that he may edit them, as he has edited other writing of this poet whom he so profoundly admires. After patient and expensive effort to obtain the letters, he learns from Tina Bordereau, Juliana's niece, that she has burned the letters "one by one," burned them obviously because he has ignored her awkward suggestion that the letters would be his if he would marry her. The final words of the story, and of the narrator who yearned to edit the letters of the poet-lover, are: "...I can scarcely bear my loss—I mean of the precious papers." These characters and others, marked by irony and isolation, have been recognized as Jamesian prototypes of the young man who is the narrator of "Portrait of a Lady" and of Prufrock as well.

In addition to the general relevance, there is a specific link between these poems and *The Aspern Papers*. The opening paragraph of James's story ends with the narrator's comment on the Bordereau house in Venice, where Jeffrey Aspern had never been—"but," says the narrator, "some note of his voice seemed to abide there by a roundabout implication and in a 'dying fall.'" The last words of the sentence, and of the paragraph, are in quotation marks, undoubtedly to signify their source in the opening lines of Shakespeare's *Twelfth Night* spoken by Duke Orsino: "That strain again! It had a dying fall." The words occur toward the end of "Portrait of a Lady"—"This music is successful with a 'dying fall'"—and again (but without quotation marks) in "Prufrock"—"I know the voices dying with a dying fall...." In each case there is certainly an echoing from Shakespeare's play, but since Eliot's poems are already associated with James's story, the twice-quoted "dying fall" becomes a roundabout echoing from that story, and from a fairly conspicuous locus of that story. If we ask why "dying fall" should be quoted in *both* poems, the quotation in *The Aspern Papers* is as good a reason, or better, than the original source in *Twelfth Night*. And if that is the case, we have not only a recurrence of echo and a confluence of echo, but an example of echoing from a source (James) which is itself the echoing of a still earlier source (Shakespeare)—a practice which we shall find to be a characteristic of Eliot's poetry.

As noted earlier, one critic, while acknowledging Eliot's disclaimer, has assumed that Browning was an influence on Eliot's poetry. Other critics have made the same assumption. There is, for example, Grover Smith's pronouncement on "Prufrock": "As a monologue it owes a good deal to Browning."[27] Kristian Smidt has reported that he "long thought the 'familiar compound ghost' of *Little Gidding* chiefly represented Robert Browning," until he was informed otherwise through direct correspondence with Eliot.[28] It is of course "Browning's mastery of the dramatic monologue" (Eliot's words)[29] which provided reason for assuming an influence. Several poems of the Prufrock group are dramatic monologues, most conspicuously "The Love Song of J. Alfred Prufrock," but also "Portrait of a Lady," "Preludes," "Rhapsody on a Windy Night," "La Figlia che Piange," and some of the shorter pieces. As in some of Browning's monologues ("My Last Duchess," "Soliloquy of the Spanish Cloister," etc.), the speakers of "Prufrock" and of "Portrait" are subject to dramatic irony. It is especially this quality of dramatic irony which relates Browning's influence with other influences so far considered.

In June, 1913, Eliot bought a copy of *Appearance and Reality* by F. H. Bradley, the British philosopher who was the subject of the doctoral dissertation which Eliot submitted to Harvard in 1916. Eliot must have already been acquainted with Bradley's work when he bought the book. Yet there is no evidence that such acquaintance existed at the time he wrote "Portrait of a Lady" and "Prufrock." But it has been a familiar fact that Bradley was a continuing influence after that time, a fact affirmed by Eliot himself: "I have written best about writers who have influenced my own poetry. And I say 'writers' and not only 'poets,' because I include F. H. Bradley, whose works—I might say whose personality as manifested in his works—affected me profoundly...."[30] One of the most frequently cited notes to *The Waste Land* is Eliot's quotation (with reference to line 412, "I have heard the key," and relevant to the words that soon follow, "each in his prison/ Thinking of the key") of this passage from Bradley's *Appearance and Reality*: "My external sensations are no less private to myself than are my thoughts or my feelings. In either case my experience falls within my own circle, a circle closed on the outside; and, with all its elements alike, every sphere is opaque to the others which surround it....In brief, regarded as an existence which appears in a soul, the whole world for each is peculiar and private to that soul."[31] Despite the post-"Prufrock" relevance of Bradley, critics have been inclined to consider Eliot's relation to Bradley by attending to "Prufrock" and other poems of that period. J. Hillis Miller's chapter on Eliot begins with the subject of Bradley and soon moves into commentary on "Prufrock" in Bradleyan terms, such as, "the reader is plunged with the first words into the spherical enclosure of Prufrock's mind....If each consciousness is an opaque sphere, then Prufrock has no hope of being understood by others."[32] In his book on Eliot, Hugh Kenner begins the chapter called "Bradley" with the words "J. Alfred Prufrock," and while there is comment on all the major poems and some others, it is "Prufrock" which is mentioned most often and which is most closely considered. Quoting the same passage from Bradley that Eliot placed in the Notes to *The Waste Land,* Kenner says that it "might have been composed by a disciplined Prufrock."[33] One could in like manner say of "Prufrock" that it might have been composed by a witty and ironical Bradley. In that kind of perspective, or retrospect, that most Laforguean poem, "Conversation Galante," is already Bradleyan.

My purpose in relating Bradley to the catalogue of influences on Eliot's early poems is to give emphasis to those qualities which the influences have in common: irony and isolation. It is also to illustrate Eliot's readiness to receive an influence, the extent to which his early work prefigures the influences that are to come, as well as those that are to increase and emerge in the course of his development. This review of influences is selective and simplified in order to show that there is a confluence of influences and that, as stated earlier, the poet himself figures in the equation of influence. It was my experience of recognizing new influence and especially new dimensions of influence which led me to recognizing also the dynamics of correspondence among the influences throughout the larger body of Eliot's poetry.

In the course of writing this book I became aware that I was experiencing *recognitions,* ideas and understandings that were new to me, and I decided to let the book develop in that way—to produce a book that would be the record of an ongoing experience. I regard this procedure as justifiable and valuable because it is so natural. The record of an experience—indeed, the very experience itself—which arrives at a recognition may be more persuasive and more interesting than a proposition which is followed by a scheme of argument and demonstration. Indeed, the experience of recognition, including the stages that lead to the recognition, is demonstration in the respect that recognition is the experience of being persuaded. There are, of course, different degrees of persuasion, ranging from full persuasion to merely "taking under consideration," and my discourse moves among these varying degrees.

It is a familiar idea that the writer (novelist, dramatist, or poet) often does not plan his "work" from beginning to end—"our beginnings never know our ends!" ("Portrait of a Lady")—but discovers the direction and the meaning of his work during the experience of creating it. This is true, I believe, of other kinds of writing as well, and I have been saying that this book is a product of that kind: the record of an ongoing experience. I should like to propose, therefore, that I have produced a commentary on T. S. Eliot's poetry which is also an experience of that poetry, still another response to it after reading it over most of a lifetime. This kind of commentary is especially appropriate to Eliot in that it reflects the ongoing aspect of his own poetry. In one of his essays Eliot stated that the entire body of a poet's work (if he is a great poet) is actually *one* poem,[34] and Eliot surely viewed his own work as such, as one poem. Yet he also acknowledged that his method of composition was one of unpremeditated accretion: "That's one way in which my mind does seem to have worked throughout the years poetically—doing things separately and then seeing the possibility of fusing them together, altering them, and making a kind of whole of them." This statement was made in an interview[35] with reference to *The Hollow Men* and *Ash Wednesday*. It is a fact, too, that *The Waste Land* and *Four Quartets* began with Eliot "doing things separately" and then seeing and making these "things" parts of a grander design.

In *Little Gidding* when the poet encounters the "familiar compound ghost," they simultaneously exclaim, "What! are *you* here?" Then the exclamation is soon followed by this comment upon it: "the words sufficed/To compel the recognition they preceded." It is my impression that this comment requires especially close attention in order to be understood, for it makes a statement that is at once precise and complex. This quality of the statement may owe something to the fact that Eliot's work-sheets show several earlier versions that are different in meaning from the final and published statement. For example, in one of these versions we find the word *pretended*, which was to be replaced by the word *preceded*—a change of word that makes for a change of meaning. Eliot explained (in a letter to John Hayward) that *preceded* was his final choice of word because it conveyed the meaning he intended: being aware of and surprised by the presence of a person before fully recognizing the person.[36] Thus the surprise— "What! are *you* here?"—precedes, compels, brings on the full recognition. It is not necessary to consider the work-sheets and the stages of revision to appreciate the account of growing awareness which is rendered by Eliot's lines, but a knowledge of that material does add emphasis to that aspect of meaning. For indeed this part of *Little Gidding* is an account of growing awareness, of finding "words I never thought to speak," as the compound ghost announces later in the passage. One of my purposes in dwelling on this subject is to indicate that *growing awareness* is also *ongoing experience*, which I acknowledge to be the nature of this book and which I would claim to be a valid and rewarding response to Eliot's poetry.

II
"A Sudden Conversion"

Much of the comment on T. S. Eliot's poetry, including some of his own comment, has been concerned with influences, sources, echoes, allusions, and so on. Consider, for example, *Four Quartets*. For a start, there is the idea that the dominant source-influence is Eliot himself—in that the five sections of *Burnt Norton* correspond to the five sections of *The Waste Land*, and that the other *Quartets* are modeled on *Burnt Norton*. I don't know who first made this observation a matter of record, but the correspondences are obvious enough and have been frequently mentioned. Another kind of source is vehemently affirmed by Harry Blamires: "'Ah, this is surely post-Joycean!' I would place *Four Quartets* first among the works which emphatically do provoke the latter response. The influence of *Ulysses* can be detected throughout the poem....*Four Quartets* is post-Joycean in that it fully reckons with the thematic development of verbal overtones which is characteristic of *Ulysses*....Eliot turned finally into the greatest Joycean of all."[1] These claims, Eliot *propre* and Joyce, are in no respect mutually exclusive. For one thing, it is widely acknowledged that *The Waste Land* is, among other things, already Joycean.[2] But there is a difference in emphasis involved. We can approach *Four Quartets* from *The Waste Land* cum Joyce, or we can prefer one approach above the other (as, between the two, I prefer Eliot *propre* to Blamires' Joyce—and it is a view which makes *The Waste Land* into a fifth and earliest Quartet). In either case, one facet of meaning is that *Four Quartets*, like Eliot's earlier work, incorporates echoes, quotations, allusions, adaptations (and so on) from a variety of sources.

There are other kinds of emphasis. For example, in 1939 I published an essay[3] observing that *Ash Wednesday* and *Burnt Norton* were informed with ideas derived from *The Dark Night of the Soul* of St. John of the Cross, and that they contained images and phrasings from that work (and I should have added, from St. John's *The Ascent of Mount Carmel* as well, from which Eliot was to quote-adapt a substantial passage in Section III of *East Coker*). More recently one critic has put *Four Quartets* in a qualified analogy with St. John: "The *Quartets* has none of the passionate excesses of *The Ascent of Mount Carmel*, but its English reserve and rationality might make it appropriate to have sub-titled it: 'The Ascent of Little Gidding.'" This is stated as a kind of "conclusion" within the essay, and then the idea is repeated as the opening sentence of the essay's final remarks: "The speaker's reflections in the *Four Quartets* have marked out a course which is an electric [*sic*; eclectic?] and poetic 'Ascent to "Little Gidding."'"[4]

Still another perspective is concerned with a special quality of style, one which several critics regard as derived by Eliot from English poets of the eighteenth century. So Hugh Kenner stated, first in an essay (1967)[5] and later in *The Pound Era* (1971), into which was fitted a slightly revised excerpt from the essay—and I quote from this book: "...Eliot when he wrote *Burnt Norton* (1935) and the rest of the *Four Quartets* (1940, 1941, 1942) went to the most inconspicuous of English poets, the ones who flourished a generation after Pope and were accustomed to take up a stance in a particularized landscape and meditate. Of all the famous poems that have preceded it *East Coker* most resembles Gray's *Elegy*, with its churches, its tombstone, its hallowed voiceless dead, its rustic intelligences. But more than it resembles a particular poem it derives from a tradition nearly anonymous...."[6] Kenner's purpose is to claim that Eliot derived an effect of anonymity by merging elements from the period styles of the English Augustans and the French *Symbolistes*. Donald Davie (in 1972) gave grateful assent to this idea—but with reservations. Kenner's "inconspicuous poets" can hardly have written "all the famous poems that have preceded...*East Coker*," so Davie observes that Kenner "is on shaky ground" when citing Gray's *Elegy*. Davie allows that "the two poems begin with strikingly similar sentiments," but he more readily associates *East Coker* with language of the Tudor period—*The Book of Common Prayer* and Sir Thomas Elyot's *Boke Named The Governour*. As for a strain of the Augustan which Davie accepts, he sees it flowing not from Gray's "marmoreal succinctness" but rather from the prosaical verse of Dr. Johnson's *London* and his *Vanity of Human Wishes*.[7]

While Kenner and Davie differ about the relevance of Gray's *Elegy* to *East Coker*, they are in general, if qualified, agreement about the Augustan ingredient throughout *Four Quartets*. Yet another critic, George T. Wright, offers the following proposition (along with detailed documentation) of a relation between Gray's *Elegy* and the entire *Four Quartets*: "There is considerable internal evidence to suggest that a possible base from which Eliot evolved *Four Quartets* is the *Elegy*.... But just as 'Gerontion' explores dimensions of religious feeling absent in Tennyson's 'Ulysses,' the *Quartets* seem almost to be going over the same ground as the *Elegy* but with an infinitely more refined instrument for sounding metaphysical and religious subtleties.... Indeed, much of the imagery of Eliot's poem echoes that of Gray's—enough to make us begin to hear the *Elegy* as prominently in the musical background of the *Quartets*. (Unconscious perhaps, but it is hard to believe that, as alert as he was to literary echoes, Eliot would, from 1934 to 1942, have remained unaware of his debt to one of the most famous poems in English....)"[8] Examples of correspondences offered by Wright are: solitary meditation on life and death within a rural landscape, tolling bells, fading light, the dust of death and decay, tombstones and their epitaphs.

On an occasion of considering that there are various views about *Four Quartets*, it occurred to me that one "might as well claim that FitzGerald's *Rubáiyát of Omar Khayyám* is a source of Eliot's poem." I have put this in quotation marks because I want to indicate that this reflection, at the time I made it, was something I would have acknowledged to be light-hearted and perhaps even light-headed. It has since, however, become a heavier kind of business. I give this account of my experience with the subject because I believe that it relates to a matter of larger interest—although it is not easy to say abruptly and briefly, what that interest is. In fact, it is an interest that I have been pursuing and will pursue, without knowing just how sharply that interest may eventually be defined. But to speak as plainly as possible at this point, my interest is in the problem of how and where to draw the line (or even an indeterminate gray area) between—how might we agree to say it?—reasonable speculations as to what might be sources and influences, on the one hand, and on the other associations (mine, Grover Smith's, Hugh Kenner's, Donald Davie's, etc.) that are incidental or aberrant or both—and I have in mind not just T. S. Eliot but all kinds of writing.

After reflecting that one "might as well claim *Omar*" I re-read *Omar*—for the first time in decades. But it is a poem we always remember, and on re-reading it I discovered that my light-hearted reflection was not so light-headed after all. I am not about to say *Ecco!* and offer an earnest and utterly persuasive demonstration that *Omar* is the source, or a source, of *Four Quartets*. The fact is that on first re-reading the poem I discovered that one might indeed "claim" *Omar* or at least "offer the suggestion" that with a thing here and a thing there seeming to correspond with things in the *Quartets*, why shouldn't it be possible to entertain the proposition, etc., etc.?

This is exactly (sort of) what I decided to do: to compose a *tour de force*—but not a farce—making the strongest possible case. But some of that purpose is already undermined and weakened, some of the *force* has gone out of the *tour*. In pursuing my first impulse, I have become persuaded that some traces (and maybe quite a few) of *Omar* can be found in the *Quartets* and in other work of Eliot. So the plot thickens. I shall be the advocate of the *Omar* source, not just within the limit of my own convictions, but as in a debating exercise, to persuade others (and perhaps, again, myself). Before proceeding, I must state my awareness that the shock of recognition, even when it is a case of mistaken identity, may propel one into a momentum of mistaken identities until real haystacks seem to bristle with needles.

My reflection was not so light-headed. We always remember *Omar*. I must have half-remembered a number of *Omar* connections with Eliot in writings by and about the poet, some of which I have since certified. For example, in a "Note" appended to his introductory Norton lecture (in *The Use of Poetry*), Eliot made the following statement: "I can remember clearly enough the moment when, at the age of fourteen or so, I happened to pick up a copy of Fitzgerald's [sic] *Omar* which was lying about, and the almost overwhelming introduction to a new world of feeling which this poem was the occasion of giving me. It was like a sudden conversion; the world appeared anew, painted with bright, delicious and painful colours."[9] This is a powerfully impressive statement, and it becomes the more powerful as it enriches and is enriched by our recognition of Eliot-FitzGerald connections. There is other conspicuous evidence that Eliot maintained a conscious interest in FitzGerald beyond the age of fourteen or so. In the Norton lecture delivered on February 17th, 1933, postulating "two hypothetical readers" while considering the problem of belief and disbelief in poets' philosophies, Eliot referred (in this order) to Dante, Lucretius, "early Buddhist scriptures," the Old Testament, and then went on to make this statement: "I can still enjoy Fitzgerald's *Omar*, though I do not hold that rather smart and shallow view of life."[10] Here, of course, Eliot was not so much reminding his audience of his own Christian belief as touching base to illustrate his point about enjoying poetry without sharing belief—so the relevance here is Eliot's abiding familiarity with and affection for *Omar*. (I shall consider later the subject of "smart" effects in Eliot's own poetry.)

There is, of course, a long and widely known Eliot-FitzGerald connection—the first two lines of "Gerontion" (1919) having been adapted with only slight change from A. C. Benson's description in his biography of FitzGerald: "Here he sits, in a dry month, old and blind, being read to by a country boy, longing for rain."[11] I had long been aware of this and had evidently assumed that it was merely incidental, presumably because others had made the same assumption. But once on the track of FitzGerald, I discovered that this has indeed been an unwarranted assumption. The assumption is itself a somewhat curious fact. Grover Smith, for example, so conscientious in attending to sources, gave only the usual passing notice to Benson, except to notice also, via Benson, a FitzGerald letter to Frederick Tennyson which tells of "an old woman in the kitchen" and "the great event of this winter is my putting up a trough round the eaves to carry off the wet," seen as a source of "The woman keeps the kitchen,..../ ...poking the peevish gutter."[12] Kenner, too, took only passing notice when in his 1959 book on Eliot, he stated that "a Life of Edward Fitzgerald provided" the old man-dry month passage—without even mentioning Benson.[13] Kenner turned briefly to the subject again in the 1967 essay from which a revised excerpt was fitted into The Pound Era. In the essay, on the same page where a resemblance between East Coker and Gray's Elegy was noted, he said "it was many years before someone—was it F. O. Matthiessen?—reading in a life of Edward Fitzgerald, discovered on the page before him the opening words of Gerontion." Again, Benson was not mentioned, but when this passage was revised for the book, the reference to Matthiessen was dropped and the FitzGerald biography is called "Benson's." In the essay Kenner went on to say, "This is not really an allusion; we are not being invited to compare Gerontion's situation with Fitzgerald's; it is an appropriated grace of expression...Eliot finds suitable...."[14] But if Kenner had returned to Matthiessen he could have been alerted to a greater relevance for Benson, and if he had turned to Benson's book he could have experienced some substantial recognition. While the Benson passage in "Gerontion" is not an allusion in the usual sense, it is (since we have no word for it) an incipient allusion, the tip of an iceberg, a clue to larger meanings in "Gerontion" and in the wider area of Eliot's work.

But first, the point about Matthiessen: in his book American Renaissance, 1941, there is a footnote where he credits Morton Zabel with having discovered the passage in Benson and he quotes from a letter (Zabel to Matthiessen) the statement that Benson's "whole book, with its picture of Fitzgerald in his pathetic, charming, and impotent old age, pondering on the pessimism of Omar, and beating out the futility of his final years, may have crystallized in Eliot's mind the situation (already drawn in earlier poems, of course) not only of 'Gerontion' but of other passages in his work of that time."[15] The same information is given in a footnote in the revised edition of *The Achievement of T. S. Eliot*, 1947, but with the latter part of Zabel's statement deleted, so that it reads, "the situation...of 'Gerontion.'"[16] Evidently Matthiessen decided to avoid the emphasis which Zabel gave to Benson's broader influence on Eliot's poetry. It is doubtful that Matthiessen made this decision based on a reading of Benson's book, for on neither occasion does he give the page number in Benson. A further irony is the fact that Eliot had revealed the source in 1938. In a short article in the English quarterly *Purpose*, Eliot neatly disposed of G. W. Stonier's assertion in a previous article that the passage in question was an imitation (and improvement) of some lines by Pound: "The line quoted from *Gerontion* was lifted bodily from a Life of Edward Fitzgerald—I think the one in the 'English Men of Letters' series."[17] Eliot didn't mention Benson, "bodily" is not quite accurate, but it was indeed that series. The information had obviously gone unnoticed by Zabel and Matthiessen and by many others down the years.

Grover Smith gives the page numbers in Benson for the dry month passage and for the Frederick Tennyson letter, and in the footnote for the latter he adds a reference to an essay called "On First Looking into Benson's *FitzGerald*" (1949) by John Abbott Clark.[18] It's my guess that Smith derived the Benson page numbers from Clark (who gives them), but it is a matter of some interest that Smith, who was so alert for and so inclusive of sources, took nothing else from Clark's essay, which abounds in "correspondences" between Eliot and Benson's *FitzGerald*. For one thing, Clark's claims are qualified by a style, especially in the final paragraphs, which deliberately mixes earnest and jest. He was reading Eliot's poems in Untermeyer. He believed that he had *discovered* the source of the dry month passage, and he relates that it was this shock of recognition which sent him re-examining Benson for correspondences in Eliot—which he found in abundance, but with an appetite at once over-eager and tentative, urging and cautioning, together and by turns. For a fair example: "I have not made this show purposelessly" is a line which for Clark "becomes much less puzzling" after he finds Benson saying, "It is true that his life seemed very purposeless."[19] Some other examples would be less remote, some even more. This may explain why Smith omitted a number of Clark's claims, suggestions, and conjectures. Some of Clark's generalizations about Benson's effect on Eliot are valid enough in essence if not in emphasis. Compared to Zabel's earlier suggestion that Benson's whole book "may have crystallized" for Eliot the situation versified in "Gerontion" and other works, Clark throws a wider net: "T.S. Eliot, especially in his early poems, was greatly influenced by Benson's *FitzGerald.*" In the course of his essay, besides "Gerontion," Clark names "Portrait of a Lady," "Prufrock," *The Waste Land, The Hollow Men,* and *Ash Wednesday.* But he does not once mention *Four Quartets* or any of Eliot's plays. Why not? Maybe he did not know these, or know them well enough. If he had, he might have made a stronger case, impressed Grover Smith more forcefully, and provided additional sources for Smith's book. A final point about Clark: he quotes from *The Use of Poetry* Eliot's statement of how FitzGerald's *Omar* gave him an "almost overwhelming introduction to a new world of feeling," and then Clark adds: "That Eliot received the initial impulse for writing *The Waste Land* from his boyhood memories of *Omar* is highly improbable." But a few sentences later he says: "*The Waste Land* might be called a twentieth-century *Omar,* in which, instead of a Loaf of Bread beneath the Bough, a Flask of Wine, a Book of Verse—and Thou, we get some tins of food, some small beer hurriedly gulped down just before closing time, a battered gramophone grinding out a cracked Shakespearean rag—and Miss Weston, with *The Golden Bough* beneath."[20] Good fun, obviously inaccurate, but no more far-fetched than some other conjectures about one poet misreading and distorting another along the road to Xanadu and other places far and near. But of FitzGerald's *Omar,* near as it was, Clark had no more to say.

Since my own setting forth on this road I have encountered A. F. Beringause's essay "Journey through *The Waste Land*" (1957) in which it is argued that "*The Waste Land* is a revamping of dramatic monologues by Edward FitzGerald and James Thomson," that in fact the main origins of Eliot's poem are FitzGerald's *Rubáiyát of Omar Khayyám* and Thomson's *City of Dreadful Night.*[21] The argument suffers from too sweeping and reductive a claim, but Beringause did call attention to a number of correspondences which I shall later note in detail.

It was my own eventual preoccupation with *Omar* which sent me, by the clue in "Gerontion," to Benson's book. I had not anticipated it would become so large a subject—large, but not so readily indicated. There is nothing else so positively taken from Benson as the "Gerontion" lines. But once we have been sensitized by the knowledge of this sure fact, we read Benson with an ear tuned for intimations of correspondence with Eliot, until one intimation and another produces so fine a tuning that what we hear is so subtly and uncertainly relevant that to communicate such recognitions we must recommend the "whole book." I agree with Zabel in the matter of "Gerontion." Although Clark hauled in some strange fish, he let some fish get away and might, I think, have cast an even wider net. With Eliot on the mind, one sees the self-mocking, the gently and ironically complaining character of FitzGerald's letters and Benson's portraiture behind the character of Gerontion, and of Prufrock too. "The life that is here proposed to depict was a life singularly devoid of incident. It was the career of a lonely, secluded, fastidious, and affectionate man." Thus opens Benson's book, with a motif that reverberates throughout the whole. One more example, near the end of the book, where Benson is describing an 1873 photograph of his subject (age 63–4): "It is a somewhat indolent face, and has an expression of vague trouble—not the face of a successful or even of a contented man....It is the face of one with great intellectual power, but dogged by a deep-seated irresolution and conscious of a certain failure of aim."[22] It is comments like these which cause Zabel and Clark and, I would think, any alerted reader to find associations with Eliot's poems—or to acknowledge them after Zabel and Clark have said *nota bene*.

Where there are several such occasions they are mutually enriching, and I would add some that are more specific and have not yet been noted. On the same page (142) in Benson as the dry month passage, just a few lines below it, there is this statement: "The old music of bygone singers, rich haunting sentences of old leisurely authors, rang in his brain, and came unbidden to his pen." Benson's language here is itself a kind of old music, and in more than one sense this old music is the very substance of Gerontion's "Thoughts of a dry brain"— "haunting sentences" certainly out of Chapman's *Bussy d'Ambois*, Lancelot Andrewes' sermon, Henry Adams' *Education*, Benson's *FitzGerald*, and possibly others. When Gerontion says that he "has no ghosts" the effect includes an irony. One of Clark's surer discoveries is Benson's report that FitzGerald used to call his youthful reader "the ghost." But Benson's comment about "haunting sentences" is, despite its old music, a clear and accurate description of Eliot's famous technique—in "Gerontion" and in poems earlier and later. No one would want to claim that Eliot got the idea from Benson or FitzGerald, but Eliot must have found (as we now do) that Benson's comment was itself a haunting sentence. There is much in Benson that has a ghostly familiarity, recalling not only the text of Eliot's verse but the technique as well. "The old music...haunting sentences...rang in his brain" is one striking example, and another is the statement (noted by Clark) that FitzGerald "used the authors whom he read somewhat like beaters, to start game in the coverts of his own mind."[23]

A justifiably wide net must provide ample room for *Omar*, but before turning to that large catch, I will select a few other things from Benson which deserve notice—starting with his comment on FitzGerald's most admired writer, Sophocles,

> who...stood apart, untouched by the fever and the dust of life, watching humanity from some serener place, lovingly and generously, but yet remotely, as a man may look down into the streets from some high tower, and see the house-roofs and the gardens, and with a kind of pity the busy little figures hurrying to and fro[24]

—so different from Eliot's "Morning at the Window" and yet so like. Another example is one of FitzGerald's letters quoted by Benson, specifically this comment on James Spedding:

> Thackeray and I occasionally amuse ourselves with the idea of Spedding's forehead: we find it somehow or other in all things, just peering out of all things: you see it in a mile-stone, Thackeray says. He also draws the forehead rising with a sober light over Mont Blanc, and reflected in the lake of Geneva. We have great laughing over this. The forehead is at present in Pembrokeshire, I believe: or Glamorganshire: or Monmouthshire: it is hard to say which. It has gone to spend its Christmas there.[25]

It is regularly observed that "Mr. Apollinax" is a portrait of Bertrand Russell, but the head in the portrait owes something to Thackeray's and FitzGerald's "great laughter" over James Spedding's forehead: "I looked for the head of Mr. Apollinax rolling under a chair./Or grinning over a screen/With seaweed in its hair."

Contrasting FitzGerald with greater poets, Benson says:

> It is hard to say how the greatest and most sensitive poets bear their grief; perhaps the secret is that, together with the intensity of suffering, they have a similarly strong power of recuperation. They descend inevitably into the dark, and when they have emerged again they can say what they have seen. But even this luxury of literary emotion was denied to FitzGerald, because he could not face the suffering that is a necessary condition of the song.[26]

Descending into the dark and emerging to report what has been seen relates with Prufrock as "Lazarus, come from the dead,/Come back to tell you all." And it relates, too, with dark descents in *Four Quartets*: "Descend lower,.../Into the world of perpetual solitude,.../Internal darkness,..." (*Burnt Norton* III), and "O dark dark dark. They all go into the dark" (*East Coker* III). If this is indeed a source, it is one that converges with others—Milton's blind Samson, Dante's dark wood, the soul's dark night of St. John of the Cross—convergences of a kind not uncommon in Eliot. In another respect, with "the suffering that is a necessary condition of the song," Benson prefigures Eliot's famous dictum of "the man who suffers and the mind which creates."

There are a number of loci of similar quality in Benson and Eliot—even in *Four Quartets* alone—and I have found it hard to know how to begin and end in indicating this large measure of correspondence, but I will give a few more examples. Just a few sentences beyond his statement about suffering and song, Benson says: "I imagine that FitzGerald's one haunting thought was regret... regret for all the beauty and charm of the world that flowered only to die.... FitzGerald lived in a wistful regret for the beautiful hours that were gone,... the sweet hour was numbered with the past even as he gazed."[27] The transitory, a central theme of *Four Quartets*, is in one instance expressed with an identical phrase: "the future is a faded song, a Royal Rose or a lavender spray/Of wistful regret for those who are not yet here to regret,/Pressed between yellow leaves of a book that has never been opened" (*Dry Salvages* III). In this usage (as, also, in "Journey of the Magi") the word *regret* has the (now rarer) meaning of nostalgic loss and not, of course, compunction.

"Other echoes/Inhabit the garden" (*Burnt Norton* I). The Benson-FitzGerald harmonic must surely be among the several strains of music, of voices and echoes which inhabit T. S. Eliot's rose-garden—as well as "the garden in the desert" (*Ash Wednesday*) where "Falls the Shadow" (*Hollow Men*). There are pages in which such voices are overhead, unsurely heard, and some where the voice is sure and clear:

> FitzGerald worshipped Scott, read and re-read him in the days of strong sight; and in the days of clouded vision had the novels read to him. Scott opened a door to him into an enchanted world, not the dreary, familiar world he knew so well and was so often wearied of, but into a brave bright country....As life went on and FitzGerald grew old he used to say that the thought, that the particular novel of Scott's which was being read to him he might never hear again, threw a little cloud of sadness over his mind.[28]

The specific correspondences are almost too obvious to cite: "the door.../Into the rose-garden..../Then a cloud passed,..." (*Burnt*

Norton I); "You bring me news/Of a door that opens at the end of a corridor,/Sunlight and singing," Harry addressing his cousin Mary in *The Family Reunion*; later in the play the long exchange with his aunt Agatha, where she says, "I only looked through the little door/When the sun was shining on the rose-garden," and he responds, "you walked through the little door/And I ran to meet you in the rose-garden."

Another source of echoes in the rose-garden (and its environs), sure and clear again:

> Omar does not go to the wine-jar only that he may forget, but that he may also remember. He feeds on honey-dew and drinks the milk of paradise that he may banish for a little the terror of the unknown, the bewildered mystery of life, the pain, the shame, the fear, and the dark shadow that nearer or further lies across the road; thus much to forget; and then he is, perchance, enabled to remember the sweet days, the spring and the budding rose; to remember that though the beginning and the end are dark, yet the God of Pain and Death is also the maker of the fair world, the gracious charm of voice and hand and eye, the woven tapestry of tree and meadow-grass, the sunset burning red behind the dark tree-trunks of the grove, the voice of music, the song of the bird, the whisper of leaves, the murmur of the hidden stream—of all the sights and sounds that fill the heart full and leave it yearning unsatisfied with the pain that is itself a joy.[29]

Benson's echoing of Coleridge has a fortuitous yet relevant accretion of meaning! Most conspicuous here is the catalogue of images in the latter half, particularly "the voice of music, the song of the bird, the whisper of leaves, the murmur of the hidden stream." Such imagery and diction reverberate in several occasions of the rose-garden as well as in closely related passages of Eliot's verse. In *Burnt Norton* (I) where the rose-garden is so prominent there is also the bird—"Quick, said the bird,...the bird called,...go, said the bird"—as well as "unheard music hidden in the shrubbery," and "leaves...full of children,/Hidden excitedly, containing laughter"—then, at the end of that Quartet, "the hidden laughter/Of children in the foliage"; in *East Coker* (III): "Whisper of running streams, and winter lightning./The wild thyme unseen and the wild strawberry,/The laughter in the garden, echoed ecstasy"; in *The Dry Salvages* (V): "The wild thyme unseen, or the winter lightning/Or the waterfall, or music heard so deeply/That it is not heard at all, but you are the music/While the music lasts"; in *Little Gidding* (V): "Through the unknown, remembered gate.../that which was the beginning;.../The voice of the hidden waterfall/And the children in the apple tree." In *The Family Reunion*, especially in the long exchange of dialogue between Harry and his cousin Mary, there are several resonances with Benson's poignant and evocative comment on Omar's resort to wine. Echoing imagery from Benson's catalogue, there is Harry's statement, "you seem/Like someone who comes from a very long distance,/Or the distant waterfall in the forest,/Inaccessible, half-heard." About twenty-five lines beyond, Mary says "Pain is the opposite of joy/But joy is a kind of pain"—so close to the final words of the passage quoted from Benson. Some moments earlier Harry has said, "other memories,/Earlier, forgotten, begin to return"—not so sharp a correspondence with the forget-remember polarity of the Benson passage, but nonetheless a recurring polarity in Eliot's verse: at the opening of *The Waste Land*—"mixing/Memory and desire,.../covering/Earth in forgetful snow"; in *Ash Wednesday*—"Rose of memory/Rose of forgetfulness"; in "Marina"—"I have forgotten/And remember"; in *Murder in the Cathedral*, where one of the better known speeches of Archbishop Thomas contains the pain-joy paradox, the forget-remember polarity, as well as intimations of themes in the Benson-FitzGerald-Omar subject:

> Peace, and be at peace with your thoughts and visions.
> These things had to come to you and you to accept them.
> This is your share of the eternal burden,
> The perpetual glory. This is one moment,
> But know that another
> Shall pierce you with a sudden painful joy
> When the figure of God's purpose is made complete.
> You shall forget these things, toiling in the household,
> You shall remember them, droning by the fire,
> When age and forgetfulness sweeten memory
> Only like a dream that has often been told
> And often been changed in the telling. They will seem unreal.
> Human kind cannot bear very much reality.
>
> (pp. 208–9)

And we recall inevitably Eliot's words on how in his youth his reading of Omar was "like a sudden conversion" introducing him to a world "painted with bright, delicious and painful colours."

III
"A Book of Verses"

This long review of the relation between Benson's *FitzGerald* and Eliot's poetry produces a number of questions (on specific points and on larger matters), some of which I will turn to eventually. But now I turn to FitzGerald's famous poem, and to my purpose of claiming that it is a major source of *Four Quartets*. The overwhelming and sudden conversion at the age of fourteen or so is a strong base on which to build, especially if we find that the effect of *Omar* on Eliot, after the first grand impact, was not altogether dormant and delayed during the earlier stages of his career. Before looking for traces or more in poetry before the *Quartets*, some general considerations are in order. *Omar* is a poem of several facets, and subject to several perspectives. In the passage quoted from Benson, of Omar going to the wine-jar in order to forget but also to remember, there is one account of the poem. In 1877, in a letter to a friend to whom he sent a copy, FitzGerald said of his poem: "*It is a desperate sort of thing, unfortunately at the bottom of all thinking men's minds; but made Music of.*" (His emphasis.) The "thing...at the bottom of all...minds" is the most common of subjects in song and story: the transitory joys of life, the inescapable effects of time and change, the certainty of death, and the mystery of it all. The stanzas of *Omar* are a lyrical meditation and reflection on the timeless subject. Although the poem begins with the rising sun and ends with the rising moon, it is, by conventional standards, loosely organized, lacking discursive progression and a firmly established continuity. FitzGerald translated freely, fitting and adapting fragments while availing himself of stylistic devices and elements from the course of English poetry up to his time. The fact that FitzGerald produced first a version of 75 stanzas, then of 110 stanzas, and finally (in third, fourth and fifth versions) of 101 stanzas is evidence of the aspect of structural looseness. The wholeness of *Omar* lies in the achieved tone that is sustained and modulated through the repetition and variation of themes and images.

As the reader no doubt suspects, I have been assuming that such description of *Omar* can be recognized as generally applicable to

Eliot's poetry, from "Prufrock" to the *Quartets*. Still another common aspect is the quality of melancholy and even of distress accompanied by effects of wit and irony. In middle-age, thirty years after his overwhelming experience, Eliot said, "I can still enjoy FitzGerald's *Omar*, though I do not hold that rather smart and shallow view of life," and he made his point. But the Epicurean view, though it may be shallow, is not essentially smart. The pleasure which readers of *Omar*, including Eliot as boy and man, find in the poem is, at least in part, an appreciation of the somberness and cleverness that attend, balance, and relieve each other. This "smartness" is very much a part of Laforgue's effect, which had such great impact on Eliot in 1908, only a few years after the impact of *Omar* (c. 1902). It is a familiar effect in Eliot up through *The Hollow Men* and *Sweeney Agonistes*, in some passages in *The Rock*, and there are instances of muted wit even in the Ariel poems, *Ash Wednesday* and *Four Quartets*. Before leaving this subject, it is worth noting that FitzGerald commented on it in the prose Introduction to the anonymous first edition (*Rubáiyát of Omar Khayyám*, 1859), saying of "The Astronomer-Poet of Persia" that "he very likely takes a humorous or perverse pleasure in exalting the gratification of Sense above that of the Intellect, in which he must have taken great delight, although it failed to answer the Questions in which he, in common with all men, was most vitally interested."[1] To restore the poem to a more familiar and more balanced perspective, there is this appropriate comment on it, made by neither FitzGerald nor Eliot: "It reads like the latest and freshest expression of the perplexity and of the doubt of the generation to which we ourselves belong."[2] Eliot spoke of *Omar* in the lectures given in 1932–33 (published as *The Use of Poetry and the Use of Criticism*) memorializing Charles Eliot Norton, friend of FitzGerald, Harvard professor, translator of Dante—Norton, who made this comment in 1888, the year T. S. Eliot was born. Was such comment ever made about *The Waste Land*? How many times?

In the critical writings on Eliot there is occasional reference to his emphatic statement about first reading *Omar*, but I have found scant notice of a possible relation between that poem and Eliot's work. Kenner in 1959, after noting that "a Life of Edward Fitzgerald" furnished the opening of "Gerontion," went on to quote this famous stanza as a statement of "resonant Stoicism [*sic*!]":

> Come, fill the cup, and in the fire of spring
> Your winter-garment of repentance fling;
> The bird of time has but a little way
> To flutter—and the bird is on the wing. (7)

Then he immediately quotes from "Gerontion": "Gull against the wind, in the windy straits," and then says—"no need to trace such sources, though since we happen to know them there is no harm in allowing them to indicate the sort of human career Eliot was contemplating when the poem formed itself."[3] A source such as FitzGerald's bird for Eliot's gull, with no supporting material besides the Benson phrases, is not persuasive, but maybe Kenner was giving expression to incipient associations between *Omar* and, not so much "Gerontion," as other poems of Eliot. An association is, in fact, made by Wright when, comparing Gray's *Elegy* and *Four Quartets*, he says that "each speaker does, in effect,... send his soul 'through the invisible' (in Edward Fitzgerald's phrase)."[4] Such large correspondence of subject in *Omar* and Eliot, especially *Four Quartets*, I have mentioned earlier and will consider again, as well as specific details. As for details, there is nothing in *Omar* like the passage from Benson which Eliot placed at the opening of "Gerontion." But there are details of various kinds, and each gains in validity as their number accumulates, until *Omar* is felt and recognized as one presence, among others, that surfaces and subsides and abides in the flow of Eliot's verse. My ultimate case and goal for this and similar propositions is *Four Quartets*, but I shall continue the preparation for that case by first pointing to details in *Omar*'s quatrains (as numbered here) and some of Eliot's earlier poems, starting with "Prufrock":

I

...among some talk of you and me

Some little talk awhile of ME and THEE (32)

II

To have squeezed the universe into a ball
To roll it toward some overwhelming question

The Ball no question makes of Ayes and Noes
But Here or There as strikes the Player goes;
And He that toss'd you down into the Field,
He knows about it all—HE knows—HE knows! (70)

III

It is impossible to say just what I mean!
But as if a magic lantern threw the nerves in patterns on a screen

We are no other than a moving row
Of Magic Shadow-shapes that come and go
Round with the Sun-illumined Lantern held
In Midnight by the Master of the Show. (68)

IV

I should have been a pair of
   ragged claws
Scuttling across the floors of
   silent seas.

And that inverted Bowl they call
   the Sky,
Whereunder crawling coop'd we live
   and die (72)

These are in an order of diminishing surface correspondence and thus provide some illustration of the variety to be considered. Example I is, even if it were mere coincidence, an almost identical pair of phrases, whereas IV is in the area of things admissible only because we (or I?) have been alerted to respond to anything of possible relevance. II and III are more complex and also more interesting. In II there is the uncommon association of questions with the rolling and tossing of balls (polo in Omar). There is a difference between the passages as to who or what is the ball and who rolls or tosses, but it is a difference which is also in the nature of a correspondence—a kind of correspondence to be discussed later. A more direct correspondence resides in the degree of intensity produced by overwhelming and the repetition of he knows. But to return to the ball (Prufrock's) for another kind of problem and a matter of some interest: it is sometimes assumed that Eliot is here echoing from Marvell's "Coy Mistress" the lines, "Let us roll all our strength and all/Our sweetness up into one ball." Yet it could, I think, more readily be claimed that he is echoing Arthur Symons' statement—"In Laforgue sentiment is squeezed out of the world before one begins to play at ball with it"[5]—and the difference here (between "squeezed...into" and "squeezed out of") is one that surely enforces the correspondence. So, we get a parcel of sources (Marvell, FitzGerald, Symons) for Eliot's ball passage, which is one among a number of instances in Eliot where there is a confluence and concinnity of multiple sources. In III the lantern is magic in one case and the shadows in another, so that we have again a correspondence in which a difference (or tension) is also present.

   My next occasion will be a sequence of three early stanzas in Omar:

> Before the phantom of False morning died,
> Methought a Voice within the Tavern cried,
>   "When all the Temple is prepared within,
> "Why nods the drowsy Worshipper outside?" (2)

> And, as the Cock crew, those who stood before
> The Tavern shouted—"Open then the Door!
>   "You know how little while we have to stay,
> "And, once departed, may return no more." (3)

Now the New Year reviving old Desires,
The thoughtful Soul to Solitude retires,
    Where the WHITE HAND OF MOSES on the Bough
Puts out, and Jesus from the Ground suspires. (4)

My first concern is the last of these stanzas (4), about which FitzGerald provides some information in his Notes.[6] The "New Year" signifies the vernal equinox: spring. The "White Hand of Moses on the Bough" FitzGerald associates with "our May-blossom," and he explains that the Persians believed that the "Healing Power of Jesus resided in his Breath." With these particulars of information I associate from "Gerontion": "In the juvescence of the year/Came Christ the tiger/In depraved May, dogwood and chestnut, flowering judas,..." Common details here are the season of spring, May and its blossom, Jesus, and blossoms named for biblical characters—Moses in the quatrain, and Judas in "Gerontion." The "depraved May" line is one of the best known of Eliot's adaptations (from *The Education of Henry Adams*), thus another example of confluence of sources, or what for the poet was a chain or cluster of associations. FitzGerald's Notes were included in all editions of the poem prepared by him and in many thereafter, which would make them available to Eliot at the age of fourteen and later.

These suppositions are strengthened when we see a relation between *The Waste Land* and this stanza (4), and then the other stanzas (2, 3) as well. Perhaps already invoked by "the New Year reviving old Desires" and by blossoms issuing from Bough and Ground is the famous opening: "April... / ...mixing/Memory and desire, stirring/ Dull roots with spring rain." Jumping to near the end of *The Waste Land* (between lines 385 and 415), we may gather a cluster of images and terms like some of those found in the stanzas. For *Omar's* "Cock crew," there is "a cock stood on the rooftree/Co co rico co co rico." For *Omar's* Temple (i.e., the Tavern, ironically) awaiting "the drowsy Worshipper outside"—"There is the empty chapel." For *Omar's* "Open then the Door!"—there is "I have heard the key/Turn in the door...." For *Omar's* "once departed, may return no more," there is the passage which tells of "our obituaries" and "our empty rooms." By this much mass and momentum, we are moved to hear *Omar's* inviting "Voice within the Tavern" echoed by the pub-keeper's contrary message (in "A Game of Chess"), "HURRY UP PLEASE ITS TIME"—and re-echoed as well from *Omar's* "You know how little while we have to stay." For *Omar's* "every Hyacinth the Garden wears" (stanza 19), there are the well-known lines which tell of the experience in the "Hyacinth garden." Several of these correspondences were noted in Beringause's "Journey through *The Waste Land*."

Another kind of correspondence occurs at the very end of the two poems. In all versions of *Omar*, just below the final stanza, is the word TAMÁM, a transliteration of the Persian word meaning *finished* or *completed*,[7] a convention comparable to FINIS or THE END below the last line of a (nineteenth or early twentieth century) novel. FitzGerald's use of the Persian word is thus a precedent for Eliot's use of the Sanskrit *shantih*, which he explains in his Notes: "Repeated as here, a formal ending to an Upanishad"—just as FitzGerald's Notes to *Omar* are a precedent for the Notes to *The Waste Land*, and the early and overwhelming encounter with *Omar* a precedent for later encounters with Eastern thought.

The door image requires more attention because, rather than a simple one-to-one relationship, it is part of an intricate pattern of multiple elements. We should recall that Benson's passage about Scott's novels opening a door for FitzGerald reverberates in several passages of Eliot's plays and *Quartets*—and so do the various doors (seven,[8] actually) in *Omar* (but this is part of the larger subject, *Omar–Four Quartets*, which we are approaching). For the present it is the door-key passage in *The Waste Land* that is relevant, and we may add, from "Rhapsody on a Windy Night," "Here is the number on the door. /Memory!/you have the key,..." and then compare one of the better known stanzas in *Omar*:

> There was the Door to which I found no key;
> There was the veil through which I might not see:
>   Some little talk awhile of ME and THEE
> There was—and then no more of THEE and ME. (32)

And from a later stanza (76), "Of my Base metal may be filed a Key/ That shall unlock the Door he howls without" (*he* being the puritanical Sufi Dervish who abstains from wine). The key is relatively incidental as compared to the larger and more generally operating door relation between Eliot and *Omar*. In this respect the door is part of a large and diffuse correspondence which may be variously represented and which at this stage I will specify as including, besides door, terms and images of desert and garden, of flowers generally and of particular kinds, and similarly of water. These are the terms and images of the rose-garden motif and of the sterility-fertility theme with its attending symbols, such as waste-land in its meaning as desert, "dead land" and "cactus land" in *The Hollow Men*, and so much in *Ash Wednesday* that, when considered and examined, poems earlier and later will be affected.

The fact is that *Ash Wednesday* is so dense with pertinences that an exhaustive account of them would produce the beginning of a combined gloss-concordance to the poem. Besides the obviously and traditionally symbolic details, there are in *Ash Wednesday* the exotic vistas, the special terrain and atmosphere which are potentially reminiscent of *Omar*, but especially the contrasting images of garden and desert which pervade Eliot's poem:

> Iram indeed is gone with all his Rose,
> And Jamshyd's Sev'n-ring'd Cup where no one knows;
> > But still a Ruby kindles in the Vine,
> And many a Garden by the Water blows. (5)

> With me along the strip of Herbage strown
> That just divides the desert from the sown,
> > Where name of Slave and Sultán is forgot—
> And Peace to Mahmúd on his golden Throne! (11)

> A Book of Verses underneath the Bough,
> A Jug of Wine, a Loaf of Bread—and Thou
> > Beside me singing in the Wilderness—
> Oh, Wilderness were Paradise enow! (12)

> Would but the Desert of the Fountain yield
> One glimpse—if dimly, yet indeed, reveal'd,
> > To which the fainting Traveller might spring,
> As springs the trampled herbage of the field! (97)

FitzGerald's note for Stanza 5 explains: "Iram, planted by King Shaddád, and now sunk somewhere in the Sands of Arabia."[9] Stanzas 11, 12 and 97 contain imagery and references by which garden and desert are associated. To be noted, also, in Stanzas 5 and 97 is the water imagery, including the word spring(s). In that most familiar of all the quatrains, the word Wilderness signifies desert. Each section of *Ash Wednesday* contains references to desert or garden or both, explicit and implicit. Most explicit, concentrated, and sharply focused is the line, "The desert in the garden the garden in the desert" (V). Some other instances to be compared with the quatrains are: "There, where trees flower, and springs flow" (I); "The single Rose/Is now the Garden" and "Under a tree in the cool of the day, with the blessing of sand, ... /In the quiet of the desert" (II); "the hawthorne blossom and a pasture scene/ ...the maytime" (III); "Who then made strong the fountains and made fresh the springs/Made cool the dry rock and made firm the sand.... /The silent sister... / ... behind the garden god, / ...But the fountain sprang up and the bird sang down" (IV); "in the desert or the rain land,/ .... /In the last desert between the last blue rocks/The desert in the garden the garden in the desert "(V)/"spirit of the fountain, spirit of the garden" (VI). Common to *Omar* and *Ash Wednesday*, obviously, is the idea of garden reverting to desert and desert to garden.

Common also is the desire and the resolve to turn away from perplexity of mind, to achieve a condition of resignation, even of liberation from vexatious concerns. In *Omar*: "Perplext no more with Human or Divine,/Tomorrow's tangle to the winds resign" (41), and "Waste not your Hour, nor in the vain pursuit/Of This and That endeavor and dispute" (54). In *Ash Wednesday* the speaker prays that he "may forget/These matters that with myself I too much discuss/Too much explain" (I); for him "neither division nor unity/Matters" (II); he achieves "strength beyond hope and despair" (III). "Teach us to care and not to care" is repeated in Sections I and VI. "Tomorrow's tangles to the winds resign" relates with "And God said/Prophesy to the wind," where Eliot takes the phrase from Ezekiel 37 and then with grim wit adds "to the wind only for only/The wind will listen." Similarly, the last two lines of *Ash Wednesday* are taken from Catholic ritual and yet constitute a correspondence (including contrast) with one of the final quatrains (99) of *Omar*:

> And even among these rocks
> Sister, mother
> And spirit of the river, spirit of the sea,
> Suffer me not to be separated
>
> And let my cry come unto Thee.
>
> Ah Love! could you and I with Him conspire
> To grasp this sorry Scheme of Things entire,
> Would we not shatter it to bits—and then
> Re-mould it nearer to the Heart's Desire! (99)

For whatever differences of tone and meaning, common to both passages is the appeal to God for comfort, for communion and fulfillment.

Earlier in these remarks I said that I would proceed to make the strongest possible case for *Omar* as a source of *Four Quartets*. A large part of that procedure has been to show how great an influence and how rich a source Benson's *FitzGerald* was for the *Quartets* and for Eliot's earlier verse as well, including the early plays—and to show that *Omar* is already echoing in Eliot's poetry before the *Quartets*. It is, I assume, evident that this procedure has been not only a preparation for the case, but has actually taken us well into the case. The rose-garden and related passages of *Four Quartets* echo from parts of Benson's book, and those parts echo directly from *Omar*. Directly relating to *Omar*, also, is the desert-garden-water imagery of *Ash Wednesday* which is part of the recurring thematic rose-garden subject in much of Eliot's verse and which enforces that facet of relation between the *Quartets* and *Omar*. Another kind of preparation was my observation that *Omar* is a lyrical meditation on the mysteries of life and death, that its wholeness and continuity derive more from the features of theme and tone and mood than from the logical progression of more conventional discourse—a description which is generally applicable to Eliot's poetry, but especially to *Four Quartets*, where there is ample discursiveness but within a larger pattern of thematic and tonal modulations.

Correspondences between the two poems are diverse, some general and pervasive, some local but recurrent and resonant, and some merely incidental and possibly coincidental. There is one subject which is the large, inclusive, and common subject of the poems, and that is Time. "Time present and time past" (I)—"Time past and time future" (II)—"Time before and time after" (III)—"time past and time future" (III)—"Time and the bell have buried the day" (IV)—"time/ Stretching before and after" (V): these phrases in *Burnt Norton* (as indicated) sound the theme that is variously represented throughout the *Quartets*. The subject of Time is so pervasive throughout these poems of FitzGerald and Eliot that an exhaustive account would indeed be exhausting, but the fact is surely evident to all who are familiar with the poems. There are, however, some points of relation between the poems which deserve more explicit and detailed notice. Corresponding to Eliot's past, present and future are *Omar*'s YESTERDAY, TODAY and TOMORROW, usually so printed and recurring (in seven stanzas) throughout the poem, as here:

> Alike for those who for TODAY prepare,
> And those that after some TOMORROW stare,
>   A Muezzin from the Tower of Darkness cries,
> "Fools, your Reward is neither Here nor There." (25)

Related to this, by concept and vocabulary, is the statement in *Burnt*

Norton (II): "I can only say, *there* we have been: but I cannot say where./And I cannot say, how long, for that is to place it in time." Further examples:

> And if the Wine you drink, the Lip you press,
> End in what All begins and ends in—Yes;
>   Think then you are TODAY what YESTERDAY
> You were—TOMORROW you shall not be less. (42)

> But if in vain, down on the stubborn floor
> Of Earth, and up to Heav'n's unopening Door,
>   You gaze TODAY, while You are You—how then
> TOMORROW, when You shall be You no more? (53)

In stanza 42 there are the terms *begin* and *end*, which comprise the opening and closing thematic phrases of *East Coker*, and which reverberate literally and essentially throughout the *Quartets*. "In my beginning is my end" and "In my end is my beginning" share an area of meaning with the statement about today, yesterday and tomorrow. Stanza 53 partakes of that meaning, too, in that *Omar* and *Four Quartets* are concerned with the question of the individual's identity in the course of time and beyond time, as in *The Dry Salvages* (III):

> time is no healer: the patient is no longer here.
> ....
> You are not the same people who left that station
> Or who will arrive at any terminus,
> ....
> You are not those who saw the harbour
> Receding, or those who will disembark.
> Here between the hither and the farther shore
> While time is withdrawn, consider the future
> And the past with an equal mind.

"While time is withdrawn" suggests the "moment in and out of time" (*The Dry Salvages*), that motif of *moments* which is so deeply significant and so markedly frequent as word and concept throughout *Four Quartets*. In *Omar* the word is not nearly so frequent (not so frequent as the concept), but it does occur:

> A Moment's Halt—a momentary taste
> Of BEING from the Well amid the Waste—
>   And Lo!—the phantom Caravan has reached
> The NOTHING it set out from—Oh, make haste! (48)

There is here a quality and substance of meaning like Eliot's many moments, such as: "the moment in the rose-garden" *Burnt Norton* (II); "the intense moment/Isolated, with no before and after" *East Coker* (IV); "the moment in and out of time" *The Dry Salvages* (V); "timeless moment(s)" *Little Gidding* (I, V). In the quatrain quoted and in others the course of time and the human condition "in the aspect of time" are represented by the symbolic imagery of travel—here by "the phantom Caravan," and in other quatrains by the "Road" (64, 80), the "Traveler" (97), and other terms of journeying. Correspondingly, in *Burnt Norton* symbolic travel imagery is the underground (subway); in *East Coker*, the "deep lane.../Into the village" and "the middle of the way" (*Nel mezzo del cammin di nostra vita*); in *The Dry Salvages*, railroad train and ocean-liner; in *Little Gidding*, "the route you would be likely to take/From the place you would be likely to come from" and "the end of all our exploring/Will be to arrive where we started."

There are some passages in which several kinds of correspondence are in close relation with each other in a single context—for example:

> Strange, is it not? that of the myriads who
> Before us passed the door of Darkness through,
>   Not one returns to tell us of the Road,
> Which to discover we must travel too. (64)

> The Revelations of Devout and Learn'd
> Who rose before us, and as Prophets burned,
>   Are all but Stories, which, awoke from Sleep,
> They told their comrades, and to Sleep returned. (65)

Clustered in the first quatrain are the motifs of travel, dark, and door. The other quatrain contains an idea like one stated earlier in *Omar*:

> Myself when young did eagerly frequent
> Doctor and Saint, and heard great argument
>   About it and about: but evermore
> Came out by the same door where in I went. (27)

> With them the seed of Wisdom did I sow,
> And with mine own hand wrought to make it grow;
>   And this was all the Harvest that I reaped—
> "I came like Water, and like Wind I go." (28)

There is in both pairs of quatrains the idea that the "wisdom" of older generations of teachers and sages, including those long dead and gone, does not yield the answers which the living questioner and quester would have—not even when the quester arrives at the age when it was expected that questions would have ripened into answers. Such an idea is stated in *East Coker* (II):

> ...the intolerable wrestle
> With words and meanings. The poetry does not matter.
> It was not (to start again) what one had expected.
> ....
> ... Had they deceived us
> Or deceived themselves, the quiet-voiced elders,
> Bequeathing us merely a receipt for deceit?
> The serenity only a deliberate hebetude,
> The wisdom only the knowledge of dead secrets,
> Useless in the darkness into which they peered
> ....
> In the middle, not only in the middle of the way
> But all the way, in a dark wood.....

This passage (with four lines and eight lines deleted, to sharpen the focus) matches in *Omar* the fruitless argument, the useless and disappointing "wisdom" of the "elders," and the symbolic (Dantean) journeying in darkness.

Quatrain 28 is of relevance in another respect, specifically "I came like Water, and like Wind I go." Each of the Quartets relates thematically with one of the four elements—air, earth, water, fire, in that order—and these are recapitulated in the refrain-like lines of the lyric at the opening of *Little Gidding* (II): "This is the death of air." "This is the death of earth." "This is the death of water and fire." Although in *Omar* there is no reference to the four elements as such, the poem has an impressive number of instances of air (wind, breath), earth (clay, dust), water (river, sea) and fire (ashes). Examples: "...even my buried Ashes such a snare/Of Vintage shall fling up into the Air" (92); "Would but the Desert of the Fountain yield/One glimpse" (97). Noteworthy here is FitzGerald's capitalization of Ashes, Air, Desert, Fountain.

There is still a large number of corresponding details to be noted. Since many of these are so obvious as to need no comment, and since they are also relatively incidental, I shall list some of these in parallel columns, following mostly the order of *Omar*'s quatrains:

Omar	Quartets
WAKE! For the Sun...	Sudden in a shaft of sunlight (*BN*, V)
...strikes The Sultan's Turret with a Shaft of Light. (1)	...the moment in and out of time, The distraction fit, lost in a shaft of sunlight (*DS*, V)

(Also, in *Murder in the Cathedral*, the line: "I have seen these things in a shaft of sunlight") (176).

Before the phantom of False morning died,
Methought a Voice within the Tavern cried (2)

In the uncertain hour before the morning.
....
And heard another's voice cry: ...(*LG*, II)

The thoughtful Soul to Solitude retires (4)

Descend lower, descend only
Into the world of perpetual solitude (*BN*, III)

Whether at Naishápúr or Babylon (7)

Whether on the shores of Asia, or in the Edgware Road. (*DS*, V)

The Leaves of Life keep falling one by one. (8)

...dust on a bowl of rose-leaves (*BN*, I)

Each Morn a thousand Roses brings, you say;
Yes, but where leaves the Rose of Yesterday? (9)

Ash on an old man's sleeve
Is all the ash the burnt roses leave. (*LG*, II)

Nor heed the rumble of a distant Drum! (13)

We cannot restore old policies
Or follow an antique drum. (*LG*, III)

...the River-Lip on which we lean—(20)

...in the sea's lips (*DS*, IV)

And many a Knot unravel'd by the Road;
But not the Master-knot of Human Fate. (31)

Into the crowned knot of fire
And the fire and the rose are one. (*LG*, V)

I think the Vessel, that with fugitive Articulation answer'd,...(36)
...wet Clay
...with its all-obliterated tongue
It murmur'd....(37)
And some loquacious Vessels were; and some
Listen'd perhaps, but never talk'd at all. (83)

....Only by the form, the pattern,
Can words or music reach
The stillness, as a Chinese jar still
Moves perpetually in its stillness. (*BN*, V)

A Hair perhaps divides the False and True;
Yes; and a single Alif were the clue—
Could you but find it—to the Treasure-house,

I said to my soul, be still, and let the dark come upon you
Which shall be the darkness of God.   As, in a theatre,
The lights are extinguished, for the

And peradventure to THE MASTER
too; (50)
Whose secret Presence through Crea-
tion's veins
Running Quicksilver-like eludes
your pains;
  Taking all drapes from Máh to Máhi;
  and
They change and perish all—but
He remains; (51)
A moment guess'd—then back be-
hind the Fold
Immerst of Darkness round the
Drama roll'd
  Which, for the Pastime of Eternity,
He doth Himself contrive, enact, be-
hold.(52)

scene to be changed
With a hollow rumble of wings, with
a movement of darkness on darkness,
And we know that the hills and the
trees, the distant panorama
And the bold imposing façade are all
being rolled away—
. . . .
I said to my soul, be still, and wait
without hope
For hope would be hope for the
wrong thing;... (EC, III)

There are other lines and points of correspondence, but this list, added to all that has gone before, reveals the extensiveness of correspondence and the various degrees of cogency. This variety illustrates how a lesser cogency is validated by a greater. For example, in the final passage of the list, Omar's "False and True" and Eliot's "hope for the wrong thing" might not be a discernible and operative correspondence if considered exclusively in their own terms. But these are drawn into the dynamics of correspondence because they adhere to a context which contains elements which are already well established. In this case, such elements are the darkness which in both poems is symbolically related to the mystery of a Reality and of a Being which are beyond the world of space and time—and, closely related to this subject, the "moment guess'd" which invokes Eliot's oft-recurring "moment." Furthermore, this manifold and pervasive motif is at once incidentally and strikingly represented in both passages by an imagery of theater: "back behind the Fold/Immerst of Darkness round the Drama roll'd" and "As, in a theatre,/...all being rolled away"—the word "rolled" providing a final touch to a pattern that may be regarded as a meaningful correspondence rather than an utter coincidence. These passages then, Eliot's and FitzGerald's, represent in small some aspects of the relationship between the two poems—of how extensively, densely, and variously Four Quartets corresponds with Omar.

The same three quatrains (50–52) will serve as a reference for other considerations. Although Omar may be regarded as Epicurean, there are also respects in which it may be seen as mystical, especially in passages such as these quatrains. We have already noted that "moment guess'd" is like Eliot's thematic "moment in and out of time." *Omar's* two lines that open with moment, I paraphrase as follows: after that special moment, God is back behind the Fold of Darkness; He is again immersed in the Darkness that is rolled round the Drama of human experience and human history—so that the Darkness of *Omar* is also Eliot's "'darkness of God." There are unquestionably differences in shades of meaning and in ultimate implications, but there is also a substantial measure of similarity. I am attending to this subject in order to emphasize that *Four Quartets* and *Omar* correspond not only in the superficial terms of words and images, but also in the deeper and embracing aspect of mystery. Whereas FitzGerald-Omar submits to mystery, in *Four Quartets* Eliot submits as a stage and step toward partaking of mystery and thus resolving it in the tradition and experience of mysticism.

The strain of mysticism in *Omar* received some emphasis from the controversy about whether the Persian author of the quatrains actually was or was not a Sufi mystic. During the interval between the first and second editions of *Omar*, "Monsieur Nicolas, French Consul at Resht" (so mentioned by FitzGerald), published a translation into French of 464 Rubáiyát (quatrains) and in his notes and comments assumed that the wine and roses and natural pleasures symbolize mystical matters—like the biblical Song of Songs, as traditionally interpreted. FitzGerald, in an addendum to the second edition of *Omar*, rejected this view and argued that Omar was "the material Epicurean that I have literally taken him for." But in the same extended comment he acknowledges that there is some ambivalence on this score: "No doubt many of these Quatrains seem unaccountable unless mystically interpreted; but many more as unaccountable unless literally."[10] Benson, too, considered this subject: "Much has been written about the symbolism of Omar." Like FitzGerald's, his interpretation is literal, but qualified, as he speaks of Omar: "He could not adopt the view that because ... delights are transitory, therefore they must be resolutely avoided.... That these things should be so sweet and yet so brief was to Omar, as to FitzGerald, the heart of the mystery...."[11] These references, to the mystical and the mystery, accord with identifications and discriminations which I make in the preceding paragraph.

The question of whether the Persian quatrains attributed to the eleventh-century astronomer-poet are in every case an expression of Sufi mysticism has been a subject of on-going contention. In 1967 a

new translation into English was published, along with critical commentaries by the collaborating translators, Robert Graves and Omar
Ali-Shah, in which FitzGerald is vehemently condemned for having
grossly misunderstood, mistranslated, and misrepresented Omar
Khayyám, whose quatrains, they assert, are unquestionably symbolic
expressions of genuine Sufi mysticism. "For four generations, indeed,
by an evil paradox, Omar Khayaam's mystical poem has been errone-
ously accepted throughout the West as a drunkard's rambling profession of the hedonistic creed: 'let us eat and drink for tomorrow we
die.'"[12] FitzGerald's "translation" may be described as rambling, but a
"drunkard's ... profession" is hardly the poem known for four generations to thousands of readers, including Charles Eliot Norton, A. C.
Benson, and T. S. Eliot. As might be expected, the claims of Graves and
Ali-Shah have been disputed (and, I believe, refuted). One of the
disputants, the Persian specialist L. P. Elwell-Sutton, makes an observation that is of general relevance to the subject: "The permeation of
so much of Persian literature by the catch-phrases of Sufism, and
conversely the use by Sufis of the stock imagery of love- and wine-
poetry, has led some students of the subject to state categorically that
all Persian poets were Sufis."[13] While I am persuaded that Omar
Khayyám was no Sufi, I have pursued the subject to this point in order
to give an emphasis to FitzGerald's own view that "many of these
Quatrains seem unaccountable unless mystically interpreted," and in
order to propose that such quatrains contributed to Eliot's youthful
response to the poem, to his enduring pleasure in it, and to the poem's
recurring, enduring, and, in fact, increasing relevance for Eliot's own
poetry. Such relevance is sustained by some information which I find
in *T. S. Eliot Between Two Worlds* by David Ward, where there is no
mention of FitzGerald or of Omar Khayyám but where there is this
statement: "...a Muslim reader may find that the image of the rose-
garden and other images associated with it recall his experience of
Sufi poetry; a Muslim acquaintance of the author's who did not know
St. Augustine, St. John of the Cross, or Lewis Carroll, Goethe or D. H.
Lawrence was able to place 'Burnt Norton' in a frame of reference
which was entirely valid for him, and may be for us, if we attend to the
echoes without prejudice."[14]

So much, then, is clear: different readers may understand *Burnt
Norton* in different terms and with different associations, while all
have understood well enough and even equally well. Perhaps—but
the question of echoes and prejudice is no simple matter. Readers of
the Persian quatrains have not found each other's readings equally
valid. Robert Graves and I, both non-readers of Persian, see the Persian

quatrains (and FitzGerald's as well) in ways that are mutually exclusive. I see FitzGerald's poem as non-Sufic but as containing "catch-phrases," "stock imagery," and indeed "echoes" of Sufi mysticism which, along with other things, are re-echoed in Eliot's poetry, especially in *Ash Wednesday* and *Four Quartets*. I have proposed, at some length and with considerable documentation, that FitzGerald's *Omar* and Benson's *FitzGerald* are a significant source of *Four Quartets*. I have said "significant" (after some reflection) so that I may ask: significant of what and to what effect?

First, I would say FitzGerald and Benson were not only the source of a number of incidental details in Eliot's poetry, but were very substantial influences—abiding and major resources of his creative activity. FitzGerald and Benson, in turn, had a shaping impact on Eliot's sensibility and imagination, on his memory, and on his developing style as a poet. After our survey of correspondences, large and small, we might with the benefit of hindsight say—How could it be otherwise?—since, at the age of fourteen or so, FitzGerald's *Omar* gave Eliot "the almost overwhelming introduction to a new world of feeling.... like a sudden conversion; the world appeared anew, painted with bright, delicious and painful colours." How could it be otherwise when reverberating through each of the *Four Quartets* and in Eliot's early (and most poetic) plays is the vivid imagery, the thematic phrasing echoed from the climactic passage in Benson's chapter on FitzGerald's *Omar*: "...the voice of music, the song of the bird, the whisper of leaves, the murmur of the hidden stream—of all the sights and sounds that fill the heart full and leave it yearning, unsatisfied with the pain that is itself a joy"? Another significance relates to the several kinds of emphasis which several critics have given to *Four Quartets*—by which I mean to say that any single emphasis, putting one claim of influence or background of correspondence or whatever above all others, is an oversimplification and a misleading view. Is the Benson-FitzGerald harmonic a lesser presence in the poem (or in its background) than Joyce, or St. John of the Cross, or Mallarmé, or Dante, or an Augustan style deriving from Gray and/or Johnson? I don't believe so. And I do believe that the Benson-FitzGerald presence in Eliot's poetry, and decidedly in *Four Quartets*, is a presence of major dimensions, and perhaps incomparable. I say "perhaps" because I am aware of being so deeply immersed in the subject, and because for so many years of attention to Eliot's poetry (and to commentary on it) I was unaware of the extent of this presence—so there may be other substantial presences, still undetected. There may arise other occasions for initiating a *tour de force* which could produce results that deserve serious consideration, even full acceptance and revised perspectives. "It is not due to any special poetical tradition; the poem is written in a grave, resonant English of a stately kind, often with a certain Latinity of phrase, and yet never really avoiding a homely directness both of diction and statement." This description, as far as it goes, is valid for *Four Quartets*, although it is Benson describing the style of FitzGerald's *Omar*.[15]

IV
Wall, Mirror, Pool

Omar was for Eliot the powerful initiation into the experience of poetry, the original and perduring influence which was a preparation and a grounds for a long and large chain and network of later influences. An immediate link in that chain, and one compounding the network, was Benson's *FitzGerald*. This book contains a striking example of influence compounding influence. I refer to the passage quoted by Benson from *Such Stuff as Dreams are made of*, FitzGerald's translation of Calderón's *La vida es sueño*, which we shall examine now in some detail.

> SEGISMUND (*within*).... Forbear! I stifle with your perfume! Cease
> Your crazy salutations! Peace, I say—
> Begone, or let me go, ere I go mad
> With all this babble, mummery, and glare,
> For I am growing dangerous—Air! room! air!
> > (*He rushes in. Music ceases.*)
> Oh, but to save this reeling brain from wreck
> With its bewildered senses!
> > (*He covers his eyes for a while.*)
> > What! Ev'n now
> That Babel left behind me, but my eyes
> Pursued by the same glamour, that—unless
> Alike bewitch'd too—the confederate sense
> Vouches for palpable: bright-shining floors
> That ring hard answer back to the stamp'd heel,
> And shoot up airy columns marble-cold,
> That, as they climb, break into golden leaf
> And capital, till they embrace aloft
> In clustering flower and fruitage over walls
> Hung with such purple curtain as the West
> Fringes with such a gold; or over-laid
> With sanguine-glowing semblances of men,
> Each in his all but living action busied,
> Or from the wall they look from, with fix'd eyes
> Pursuing me; and one most strange of all
> That, as I pass'd the crystal on the wall,
> Look'd from it—left it—and as I return,

Returns, and looks me face to face again—
Unless some false reflection of my brain,
The outward semblance of myself.—Myself?
How know that tawdry shadow for myself,
But that it moves as I move; lifts his hand
With mine; each motion echoing so close
The immediate suggestion of the will!
In which myself I recognise—Myself!—
What, this fantastic Segismund the same
Who last night, as for all his nights before,
Lay down to sleep in wolf-skin on the ground
In a black turret which the wolf howl'd round,
And woke again upon a golden bed,
Round which as clouds about a rising sun,
In scarce less glittering caparison
Gather'd gay shapes that, underneath a breeze
Of music, handed him upon their knees
The wine of heaven in a cup of gold,
And still in soft melodious under-song
Hailing me Prince of Poland!—"Segismund,"
They said, "Oh, welcome, welcome to his own,
Our own Prince Segismund."[1]

As a source of "A Game of Chess," the passage is remarkable in a number of respects. Among all the sources echoed in "A Game of Chess," FitzGerald's "Segismund" speech (as I shall call it) is by far the most extensive, supplying numerous and various echoes "in rich profusion." "Segismund" is about fifty lines long (counting the stage directions), and it is echoed in "A Game of Chess" from "perfume" of the first line to "soft melodious under-song" (corresponding to Eliot's nightingale) near the end. Although most of the echoes are from the first half of "Segismund," they are obviously distributed at random throughout the first thirty to fifty-five or so lines of "A Game of Chess"—since "My nerves are bad tonight," etc., through "What shall we ever do?" appear as an expanded echoing of "crazy salutations.... I go mad ... this babble, mummery.... this reeling brain ... its bewildered senses." Some other echoed elements (not yet mentioned) are "*He covers his eyes....* bright-shining floors ... the stamp'd heel ... marble-cold ... clustering flower and fruitage ... semblances of men ... from the wall they look from, with fixed eyes/Pursuing me ... the crystal on the wall ... glittering caparison ... a breeze/Of music." Immediately following quotation of "Segismund," Benson makes a brief comment of three sentences, and I quote the last two: "We feel that it is neither FitzGerald nor Calderón. It is accomplished and stately, but there is a want of dramatic sympathy, a want of fire and glow for which no execution, however careful, can atone."[2] Clearly this "fire and glow" has entered the chorus of echoes, specifically where the woman's brushed hair "Spread out in fiery points/Glowed into words, then would be savagely still."

When Benson said "We feel that it is neither FitzGerald nor Calderón," he referred in general to FitzGerald's translations of Calderón's plays, and also to the "Segismund" passage. In the latter respect Benson's comment can justly be called pregnant with meaning, probably more so than even Benson was aware (and he was aware of much). My own meaning will emerge as we confront some obvious questions. How can we account for Eliot's echoing, at once extensive and concentrated, from an excerpt quoted by Benson, from a play that Eliot had probably never read? By the end of the nineteenth century the published translation (*Two Dramas from Calderón*, 1865; *The Mighty Magician* from *El mágico prodigioso* and *Such Stuff as Dreams are made of* from *La vida es sueño*) was already a rare collectors' item—the edition had been only "about a hundred copies."[3] Moreover, the entire passage has no equivalent in the Spanish but was invented by FitzGerald and, in his "free translation," placed in an appropriate scene of the play. As Benson said, it is not Calderón. It appears, then, that the passage had sunk into Eliot's memory and dissolved, and in this case was reconstituted and surfaced, as we find it in "A Game of Chess." The echoes and allusions indicated by Eliot in his Notes, as well as others that have come to light, are related to "Segismund" by a multi-dimensional complexity. One of my meanings here is that Eliot echoes "Segismund" not only with details that are apparent on the surface of both passages but also in a dimension that is beyond the surface. I shall begin to explore this large and complex subject with this example: "the glass/Held up by standards wrought with fruited vines" corresponds with (besides "the crystal on the wall")

> airy columns marble-cold,
> That, as they climb, break into golden leaf
> And capital, till they embrace aloft
> In clustering flowers and fruitage....

This imagery of upward thrusting "fruited vines" and "flowers and fruitage" is related to the "sylvan scene"—derived, as Eliot's note states, from Milton's *Paradise Lost*,[4] Book IV:

>   *overhead up grew*
> Insuperable heighth of loftiest shade,
> Cedar, and pine, and fir, and branching palm,
> A *sylvan scene*, and as the ranks *ascend*
> Shade above shade, a woody theater
> Of stateliest view. Yet higher than their tops
> The verdurous wall of Paradise *up sprung*
> Which to our general sire gave prospect large
> Into his nether empire neighboring round.
> And *higher* than that wall a circling row
> Of goodliest *trees loaden with fairest fruit*,
> *Blossoms and fruits* at once of *golden hue*
> Appeared, with gay enameled colors mixed;...
>   (ll. 137–149; italics added, here and hereafter)

Such imagery of upward branching trees with golden fruit and flowers occurs soon again in Book IV:

>   the Tree of Life,
> High eminent, blooming *ambrosial fruit*
> Of *vegetable gold*,...
>   (ll. 218–220)

> Groves whose rich trees wept odorous gums and balm,
> Others whose fruit *burnished* with *golden* rind
> Hung amiable....
>   (ll. 248–250)

>   the *mantling vine*
> Lays forth her *purple grape*, and gently creeps
> Luxuriant;...
>   (ll. 259–260)

>   the roof
> Of thickest covert was inwoven shade
> Laurel and myrtle, and what higher grew
> Of firm and *fragrant* leaf; on either side
> Acanthus, and each *odorous* bushy shrub
> Fenced up the verdant wall; each beauteous
>   flow'r,
> Iris all hues, roses, and jessamine
> *Reared high* their flourished heads between, and
>   wrought
> Mosaic;...
>   (ll. 692–700)

There is a sense in which Eliot's use of "sylvan scene" invokes *all* of

Paradise Lost, but especially Book IV where Adam and Eve (already spied on by Satan) are pictured in their unfallen state, within a "sylvan scene" described in rich and elaborate detail.

At this point I am ready to propose that there are several lines of echoings, lines running separately and lines merging and weaving among each other. The passages already quoted show this in some measure. The upward branching and fruit-laden imagery of Book IV is echoed in "Segismund," and from "Segismund" such imagery is echoed by Eliot. It may be noted that in Milton there are natural details which are described as prefiguring man-made objects such as "woody theater," "verdurous wall" and "verdant wall," and the flowers which "wrought/Mosaic"—whereas in "Segismund" and in Eliot the images are fabricated simulations of nature. Relevant to this artificial splendor is the perfume, stifling in "Segismund" and synthetic in Eliot, corresponding and contrasting with the natural fragrances of Book IV. Examples from the passages quoted above are "ambrosial fruit," "odorous gums and balm," "fragrant leaf" and "odorous bushy shrub." More such fragrant imagery follows only fifteen lines beyond "sylvan scene":

> now gentle gales
> Fanning their *odoriferous* wings dispense
> *Native perfumes,* and whisper whence they stole
> Those balmy spoils. As when to them who sail
> Beyond the Cape of Hope, and now are past
> Mozambic, off at sea northeast winds blow
> Sabean *odors* from the spicy shore
> Of Araby the Blest, with such delay
> Well pleased they slack their course, and many a
> league
> Cheered with the *graceful smell* old Ocean smiles.
> So entertained those *odorous sweets* the Fiend.
> (ll. 156–166)

"Native perfumes" means, of course, natural fragrances as distinguished from "synthetic perfumes."

But to turn directly to the matter of the lines of echoing. I am proposing that the perfume imagery of Book IV is echoed in "Segismund" and then from there it is echoed by Eliot. But I am also proposing that, through the detail of the "sylvan scene," the perfume imagery of Book IV is *directly* echoed by Eliot. Thus a cluster of images (branching trees, fruit, perfume) echoes in "A Game of Chess" from Book IV and it re-echoes, with acquired qualities, from "Segismund."

At this stage I am not concerned with possible distinctions between conscious and unconscious echoes, although the question is one which attends the observations that I have been making and those which I shall proceed to make. Conscious or unconscious, FitzGerald's echoing of Book IV is not arbitrary and unaccountable. In Calderón's play Segismund, Prince of Poland, is an Edenic character and a kind of "wild child." Because of astrological signs preceding and following the Prince's birth, his father King Basil, fearing he has sired a monstrous creature, arranges for the child to be kept in a dungeon tower located in a remote wilderness. By the time the Prince is a young man, the King decides to "test" him after all and has him brought in a trance to the royal palace. It is at this point in the play that Segismund, having roused from his trance, gives expression to his amazement and confusion—in a speech elaborated by FitzGerald beyond Calderón's text. On first reading the speech in Benson, I was struck by the correspondences with "A Game of Chess." It was later that I became aware by stages of the intricate interrelationship among Book IV, "Segismund," and Eliot. This awareness was initiated by the mirror experience in "Segismund":

> semblances of men,
> Each in his all but living action busied,
> ....
> ...and one most strange of all
> That, as I pass'd the crystal on the wall,
> Look'd from it—left it—and as I return,
> Returns, and looks me face to face again—
> ....
> ...it moves as I move; lifts his hand
> With mine;...

This reminded me of Eve's mirror experience in Book IV as she first looked into the lake:

> As I bent down to look, just opposite,
> A shape within the wat'ry gleam appeared
> Bending to look on me, I started back,
> It started back, but pleased I soon returned,
> Pleased it returned as soon with answering looks.
> (ll. 460–464)

This correspondence reminded me in turn that "sylvan scene" was in Book IV, and thereafter, re-reading everything, I became persuaded that the Milton-"Segismund"-Eliot correspondences are multiple and intricate—so much so that they can be fully appreciated, beyond my exposition, only by an alert reading. From such reading, according to my own experience, there emerges an awareness of the density of associations which lie behind the allusions and echoes which are on the surface of "A Game of Chess." Eliot includes "the glass" which "Doubled the flames of sevenbranched candelabra," but this is not the mirror experience of Book IV and of "Segismund." Yet this mirror experience sharpens and extends the associations which emanate from "sylvan scene" and is a constituent of that current of influence and of meaning which arrives in "A Game of Chess" directly from Book IV and indirectly from "Segismund." Part of the meaning here is the ironic contrast between the unfallen world of Adam and Eve and the world of the man and woman who "shall play a game of chess" and of Lil and Albert—even if, in another perspective, there is the meaning that *Paradise Lost* and Genesis are among "other withered stumps of time." So to consider is to move toward the idea that not only are the overt allusions a part of Eliot's poem, but that the associative process—and all elements that may come to be recognized as operating within this process—is itself part of the poem. This is a matter to which I shall return later at greater length.

The mirror experience is a line of echoing from Book IV to "Segismund," but it does not specifically continue into "A Game of Chess." Now I would indicate an echoing direct from Book IV to Eliot which has no specific reverberation in "Segismund." I refer to "The glitter of her jewels.../From satin cases poured in rich profusion"—and to that part of Book IV which tells of the fountain in Eden which eventually produces "four main streams"

> wand'ring many a famous realm
> And country whereof here needs no account,
> But rather to tell how, *if art could tell*,
> How from that *sapphire* fount the crispèd brooks,
> Rolling on orient *pearl* and sands of *gold*,
> With mazy error under pendant shades
> Ran nectar, visiting each plant, and fed
> Flow'rs worthy of Paradise which *not nice art*
> In beds and curious knots, *but nature boon*
> *Poured* forth *profuse* on hill and dale and plain.
> (ll. 234–243)

The corresponding elements here, as indicated, are *sapphire, pearl, gold, poured, profuse*. I have emphasized some other phrases in the passage—"if art could tell" and "not nice art...but nature boon"—because they are relevant to that theme of difference between synthetic and natural, artifice and nature, for the flower and fruitage of "Segismund" rise from columns marble-cold, and in "A Game of Chess" the fruited vines are wrought and the dolphin is carved.

So far I have been examining interrelationships among "A Game of Chess, "Segismund," and Book IV of *Paradise Lost*. Now I shall consider how these interrelationships relate with other allusions and echoes in Eliot's poem, where the most conspicuous allusion is of course the echoing, by the opening lines, of Enobarbus' famous speech in *Antony and Cleopatra*:

> The barge she sat in, like a burnish'd throne,
> Burn'd on the water. The poop was beaten *gold*;
> *Purple* the sails, and so *perfumed* that
> The *winds* were lovesick with them; the oars were silver,
> Which to the *tune of flutes* kept stroke, and made
> The water which they beat to follow faster,
> As amorous of their strokes. For her own person,
> It beggar'd all description. She did lie
> In her pavilion, cloth-of-gold, of tissue,
> O'erpicturing that Venus where we see
> The fancy outwork nature. *On each side her*
> *Stood pretty dimpled boys, like smiling Cupids,*
> With divers-colour'd fans, whose wind did seem
> To glow the delicate cheeks which they did cool,
> And what they undid did....
> Her gentlewomen, like the Nereides,
> So many mermaids, tended her i' th' eyes,
> And made their bends adornings. At the helm
> A seeming mermaid steers....
>   ...From the barge
> *A strange invisible perfume hits the sense*
> Of the adjacent wharfs.
>   (II. ii. 195–217)

It has been noted that, besides the opening lines, Eliot echoes also the perfume and the Cupids. But when we are aware of "Segismund" and Book IV, we can recognize other details which are part of the rich field of interrelationships, some of these details lying outside the surface-text of "A Game of Chess." Such are the gold and purple, which occur also in "Segismund":

In clustering flower and fruitage over walls
Hung with such *purple* curtain as the West
Fringes with such a *gold*;...

Gold and golden references abound in Book IV, in two instances along with purple, as in the description of the sun

Arraying with reflected *purple* and *gold*
The clouds that on his western throne attend
(ll. 596–7)

and in the celebration of wedded love, which includes mention of the mythical deity (Cupid!):

Here Love his *golden* shaft employs, here lights
His constant lamp, and waves his *purple* wings
(ll. 763–4)

In the immediate context of each of these passages are references to the nightingale and her song—in the first instance, "the wakeful nightingale/...all night long her amorous descant sung" (602–3), and in the second, Adam and Eve "lulled by nightingales, embracing slept" (771).

A group of images common to all contexts (Eliot, Enobarbus, Segismund, Book IV) is that of perfume, wind, and music, although not in every case in immediate relation. Since the perfume imagery is evident enough, I will take notice of it only when it is closely involved with the other kinds of imagery—as it is in Book IV, where the wind is both audible and fragrant:

...now gentle gales
Fanning their odoriferous wings dispense
Native perfumes, and whisper whence they stole
Those balmy spoils.
(ll. 156–9)

The birds their choir apply; airs, vernal airs,
Breathing the smell of field and grove, attune
The trembling leaves,...
(ll. 264–6)

Toward the end of "Segismund" there is the striking locution "a breeze/Of music," and Eliot describes "odours" as "stirred by the air/That freshened from the window"—only a few lines before the inviolable voice of the nightingale is mentioned. Two kinds of imagery are merged in "a breeze of music." In "airs, vernal airs" there is a triple merging—of breeze, smell, and music. Enobarbus tells of wind-borne perfume and of the music of wind-instruments ("the tune of flutes").

Although in the opulent boudoir of "A Game of Chess" there are no attending servants, this is a kind of imagery which recurs in the other contexts and which is thus a part of what we find to be an even larger and more detailed web of associations. Enobarbus describes Cleopatra's attendants as ornaments in that ornate barge scene:

> Her gentlewomen, like the Nereides,
> So many mermaids, tended her i' th' eyes,
> And made their bends adornings.

Toward the end of "Segismund," the Prince of Poland awakes from his trance in surroundings no less sumptuous than Cleopatra's pavilion and as lavishly attended:

> And woke again upon a golden bed,
> Round which as clouds about a rising sun,
> In scarce less glittering caparison,
> Gather'd gay shapes that, underneath a breeze
> Of music, handed him upon their knees
> The wine of heaven in a cup of gold,
> And still in soft melodious under-song
> Hailing me Prince of Poland!

Servants and served are compared here to clouds and rising sun. In Book IV clouds and setting sun are in an obverse comparison, where the sun is described as

> Arraying with reflected purple and gold
> The clouds that on his western throne attend.
> (ll. 596–7)

It can hardly be claimed (although it might be speculated) that Enobarbus' speech is echoed in Book IV and then echoed and re-echoed in "Segismund." But it has been indicated that when we recognize the relationship of "Segismund" and "A Game of Chess," then multiple and mutual echoings and re-echoings may also be recognized, so that the FitzGerald-Eliot relationship comes to be seen as far more than a one-to-one relationship. As we have seen, and shall see further, "Segismund" was for Eliot the basis of a continuum of associations and echoes, one reason being that "Segismund" is itself comprised of echoes.

In *The Tightrope Walkers* Giorgio Melchiori has a chapter "Echoes in 'The Waste Land'" where he credits (too readily) Laura Riding and Robert Graves with having "pointed out one poem which has largely contributed to the imagery of 'A Game of Chess': Keats' *Lamia*."[5] Before commenting on particulars of this matter, I shall quote from *Lamia*[6] (Part II) some passages, obviously relevant to my purpose, which describe the scene of a wedding banquet:

> Fresh carved cedar, mimicking a glade   125
> Of palm and plantain, met from either side,
> High in the midst, in honour of the bride:
> Two palms and then two plantains, and so on.
> From either side their stems branch'd one to one
> All down the aisled place; and beneath all   130
> There ran a stream of lamps straight on from wall to wall.
> So canopied, lay an untasted feast
> Teeming with odours. Lamia, regal drest,
> Silently paced about, and as she went,
> In pale contented sort of discontent,   135
> Mission'd her viewless servants to enrich
> The fretted splendour of each nook and niche.
> Between the tree-stems, marbled plain at first,
> Came jasper panels; then anon there burst
> Forth creeping imagery of slighter trees,   140
> And with the larger wove in small intricacies.
> Approving all, she faded at self-will,
> And shut the chamber up, close, hush'd and still,...   143
>
>   Of wealthy lustre was the banquet room   173
> Fill'd with pervading brilliance and perfume:
> Before each lucid pannel fuming stood   175
> A censer fed with myrrh and spiced wood,
> Each by a sacred tripod held aloft,
> Whose slender feet wide-swerv'd upon the soft
> Wool-woofed carpets; fifty wreathes of smoke
> From fifty censers their light voyage took   180
> To the high roof, still mimick'd as they rose
> Along the mirror'd walls by twin clouds odorous.
> Twelve sphered tables, by silk seats insphered,
> High as the level of a man's breast rear'd
> On libbard's paws, upheld the heavy gold   185
> Of cups and goblets, and the store thrice told

Of Ceres' horn, and, in huge vessels, wine
Come from the gloomy tun with merry shine.
Thus loaded with a feast the tables stood,
Each shrining in the midst the image of a God.   190

When in an antechamber every guest
Had felt the cold full sponge to pleasure press'd,
By minist'ring slaves, upon his hands and feet,
And fragrant oils with ceremony meet
Pour'd on his hair, they all mov'd to the feast   195
In white robes, and themselves in order placed
Around the silken couches, wondering
Whence all this mighty cost and blaze of wealth could spring.

Soft went the music the soft air along,
While fluent Greek a vowel'd undersong   200
Kept up among the guests,...

Melchiori too readily credits Riding and Graves with recognizing Eliot's echoing of Keats's imagery, for they were concerned to claim for Eliot "an improvement on all previous treatments of a favorite refined topic—perfumes," and they quote from *Lamia* lines 173–182.[7] Melchiori, quoting lines 173–198, finds a detailed echoing: "Here are the perfumes which, as in Eliot, and Shakespeare's barge scene, play such an important part in the heightening of the sensuous atmosphere; here are the mirrors, reflecting the smoke of the censers.... Gold, fragrant oils, exquisite words, the idea of pouring giving a sense of affluence: all these are used by Eliot and Keats in exactly the same way, conveying a sense of untold magnificence with a shadow lurking somewhere amidst the profuse beauty of the scene. And not only the tone, but the full rhythm of Eliot's lines is very close to Keats'."[8] I have quoted still more of *Lamia* because this larger context clearly contains elements which, along with those noted by Melchiori, belong to that continuum of associations which extends through "A Game of Chess" and, with a special emphasis, through "Segismund." For example, there are the facsimiles of nature: "carved cedar, mimicking a glade/Of palm and plantain" (ll. 125–6), "tree-stems, marbled plain" (l. 140). If *Lamia* flows into "A Game of Chess," then "Segismund" may be the channel through which it flows. This is to suggest that in "Segismund" FitzGerald is actually echoing *Lamia*, in which case it could be said that FitzGerald is echoing Keats-cum-Milton, just as it could be said that in "A Game of Chess" Eliot is echoing A-cum-B-cum-C-cum-D and so on.

As in other cases, it is the variety and accumulation of details which are persuasive. On this score, I call attention again to "a breeze of music" and "soft melodious under-song," and the final lines of my quotation from *Lamia*:

> Soft went the music the soft air along,
> While fluent Greek a vowel'd undersong
> Kept up among the guests,...

The similarity of meaning and imagery and the common use of the uncommon word *undersong* enhance the possibility that FitzGerald is indeed echoing Keats. This same passage is quoted admiringly by Douglas Bush in his *Mythology and the Romantic Tradition in English Poetry* (1937), and he was impressed enough by *undersong* to remark in a footnote that the word "might have come from the homely Wordsworthian 'kettle whispering its faint undersong' (*Personal Talk*, i); cf. Spenser, *Prothalamion*, l. 110." So the word is noteworthy in more than one sense. On the same page (113), Bush quotes from *Lamia* the same lines that Riding and Graves had quoted earlier, as well as some additional lines quoted later by Melchiori. Bush's purpose here is to offer what he calls his "ewe-lamb of research," by which he means his proposition that for *Lamia* Keats's source of "information about ancient manners and furniture" was John Potter's *Archaeologia Graeca*. Bush does not mention Eliot in his discussion of *Lamia*, but he touches my subject with his remark (p. 114, n. 49) that "details of Keats's feast suggest Virgil (*Aen.* i. 701 ff., 723 ff.)," for this reference includes Eliot's note to "laquearia": "*Aeneid*, I, 726." Bush means, of course, that he finds Keats echoing not only Potter's *Archaeologia Graeca* but Virgil's description of the banquet-hall in which Aeneas was feasted by Dido. He is more explicit on this point when, later in the book (p. 515) he comments on "A Game of Chess" and provides (again) a relevant footnote: "The resemblance which has been noticed (Matthiessen, pp. 85, 94) between these lines and Keats's picture of the banquet-hall in *Lamia* may be partly explained by the fact that Keats evidently recollected, along with other things, the Virgilian passage to which Eliot explicitly refers (see above, Ch. III, note 49)." Just a bit farther along in the same paragraph Bush resorts to still another footnote for recording his cautious (and impressively early) insightfulness: "The phrase 'withered stumps of time,'... suggests the repeated allusions to the 'stumps' of the ravished and mutilated Lavinia and her use of Ovid's story of Tereus (*Titus Andronicus*, II. iv. 4, III. ii. 42, V. ii. 183). But the phrase describes other old pictures on the walls, and, since the poet has just cited the first book of Virgil, one may think of the pictures at which Aeneas gazed, pictures of heroic action. Such queries may be quite fanciful, but Mr. Eliot awakens many echoes, whether always consciously or not." One may think also of pictures on the wall in "Segismund." As for "withered stumps of time," I would not dispute the association with Lavinia. But another association (my own, and possibly Eliot's, consciously or not) could be that body of arboreal imagery in "Segismund," *Paradise Lost,* and *Lamia,* from which the "fruited vines" of "A Game of Chess" derive and perhaps, too, the "withered stumps of time." It is the pictures (and more precisely, the subjects pictured) which are "told upon the walls," so that the "sylvan scene," by which Milton signifies his description of the Garden of Eden, is referred to as one among a number of "withered stumps." What is, or was, a "sylvan scene"—Milton's telling of the story of Eden, Ovid's telling of the story of Philomel, all once meaningful and beautiful myths and legends—has withered and been reduced to stumps. With "other withered stumps of time" Eliot quite consciously represents the idea of awakening many echoes.

It is a commonplace of scholarship that *Paradise Lost* reflects Milton's knowledge of a vast and varied body of literature. "Milton's ostensible task was to make the earthly paradise in Book IV perfect and delightful, and out of allusions to and reminiscences of almost every Biblical, classical, modern, and 'real' garden he could find, he composed his own complete, integrated vision." So states A. Bartlett Giamatti in *The Earthly Paradise and the Renaissance Epic.* A garden to which Giamatti gives special attention as a source for Milton's Eden is the Bower of Bliss in Spenser's *The Faerie Queene* (II. xii. 42–87).[9] This source requires our attention, too, because we find there the familiar arboreal imagery, as well as other relevant elements. Spenser describes the Bower as a place

> In which what euer in this worldly state
> Is sweet, and pleasing vnto living sense,
> Or that may dayntiest fantasie aggrate,
> Was poured forth with plentiful dispence,
> And made there to abound with lauish affluence. (42)

Although the Bower has no walls with pictures, it has an ivory gate on which "all the famous history/of *Iason* and *Medaea* was ywrit" (44), much of which is detailed in this and the next stanza (45) and then summarized with the statement, "All this, and more might in that

goodly gate/Be red" (46). As for arboreal imagery, it is encountered by
Sir Guyon:

> he came unto another gate,
> No gate, but like one, being goodly dight
> With boughs and branches, which did broad dilate
> Their clasping armes, in wanton wreathings intricate. (53)

> So fashioned a Porch with rare deuice,
> Archt ouer head with an embracing vine,
> Whose bounches hanging downe, seemed to entice
> All passers by,... (54)

> And them amongst, some were of burnisht gold,
> So made by art, to beautifie the rest,
> Which did themselues emongst the leaues enfold. (55)

By now we find this imagery of boughs and branches familiar enough,
and we notice too that in Spenser's Bower of Bliss there is an inter-
mingling of genuine vegetation with simulations: "some were of
burnisht gold,/So made by art, to beautifie the rest,"—and to symbolize the deceitful and unnatural temptations to sin and perdition
proffered by the Bower of Bliss.

I have reviewed familiar material by and about Milton and Spenser
as a way of approaching the observation that in "A Game of Chess" one
of Eliot's purposes was indeed to "awaken many echoes," and that this
purpose was moreover to echo precisely those sources which are
themselves the established touchstones of rich and multiple echoings, overlapping garden and banquet scenes, in Milton and Spenser,
Ovid and Virgil, on back to Homer and the ultimate antiquities. If
critics have been more or less aware that *echo* is itself an underlying
theme of "A Game of Chess," then the "Segismund" connection
underlines that theme and sharpens our awareness of it.

Even "The Chair she sat in, like a burnished throne" is a secondary
echo, for it is well known that Shakespeare's purple passage is at once
a brilliant and close re-working of a passage in North's translation of
Plutarch. As for ultimate antiquity, there is the sevenbranched can-
delabrum (doubled to plural form, candelabra, by the mirror). I am
persuaded (by David Ward)[10] that this Jewish menorah is intended as
an echoing of Exodus 25–27 where the Lord's instructions to Moses
for furnishing the tabernacle include oils, incense, perfume, precious
stones and precious metal, ornamental hangings, and other opulent

details such as are paralleled by the boudoir of "A Game of Chess" and by the banquet halls and gardens that have preceded it. Exodus 25 (KJV):

> 6 Oil for the light, spices for anointing oil, and for sweet incense,
> 17 And thou shalt make a mercy seat of pure gold:...
> 18 And thou shalt make two cherubim of gold...in the two ends of the mercy seat.
> 31 And thou shalt make a candlestick of pure gold:...
> 32 And six branches shall come out of the side of it; three branches of the candlestick out of the one side, and three branches of the candlestick out of the other side.

Because the lady's boudoir is already so crowded with elements from multifarious sources, I am convinced that the "mercy seat" (otherwise known as the throne of God) and its accoutrements are among these sources. Conspicuous in the biblical inventory are the two cherubim, corresponding to the Cupidons of the boudoir (and to the "smiling Cupids" of Shakespeare's barge scene). Relevant also is the fact that the "Chair" she sat in is capitalized in all editions of The Waste Land, so that I find this capitalization enforcing the allusion to the sanctum sanctorum of tabernacle (and temple). With this emphasis on "Chair," it may be recalled that in French the word so spelled means flesh. Such an embittered pun would fit David Ward's proposition that the ironical matching of temple and boudoir includes an irony deriving from the Christian idea of the human body as temple. In any event, "sevenbranched candelabra" is like "laquearia" and "sylvan scene" in that these are all small windows which give upon broad vistas of allusion, of meaning, and of processes poetic and psychological.

V
The Mirror Experience

"Segismund" is interesting and important as a source in a special way: the passage itself has an ambience of sources, and "A Game of Chess" is even more strikingly possessed of such ambience. This quality is made more evident through our recognition of "Segismund" for the kind of source it is. It was so for me. The mirror experience in "Segismund" sent me to Eve's mirror experience in Book IV of *Paradise Lost* and from there to an expanding network of correspondences for both "Segismund" and "A Game of Chess." It is, obviously, my associations as a reader which lead me to indicate associations within the poem—and, presumably, within the mind and poetic processes of T. S. Eliot. I make this observation so that it may serve as a safeguard against oversimple and reductive conclusions—for myself and for my reader—and so that I may proceed with further associations.

I use the mirror experience as an illustration because it has served, again, for an association. It reminded me of Joseph Conrad's long short story "The Return" (contained in *Tales of Unrest*, 1898). The fact is that I was already aware of a relation between that story and "A Game of Chess." In 1950 Robert L. Morris published a very short article[1] claiming the final scene of that story as a substantial source of "the first fifty lines" of "A Game of Chess," and he quotes three passages[2] from that scene to indicate "parallels, both in image and tone between Conrad's prose and Eliot's poetry." In one of these passages the closest parallels are "the discreet reserve of walls, of closed doors, of curtained windows.... the mutilated immortality of famous bas-reliefs.... the woman of marble, composed and blind on the high pedestal,... with a cluster of lights"—and in another passage, among the furnishings described, an actual man and woman: "Her hair streaming on her shoulders glinted like burnished gold. He looked into the unfathomable candour of her eyes. Nothing within —nothing—nothing." The parallels here, as Morris notes, are the streaming hair, burnished gold, and the repetition of "nothing." I discovered Morris's short but impressive and persuasive article over two decades ago when I was working on my essay "Laforgue, Conrad, and T. S. Eliot." There I discuss at length *Heart of Darkness* as one of Eliot's major sources, and then in my "After-Notes" I refer to "The Return," from which I quote the sentence, "He was afraid with that penetrating faltering fear that seems, in the very middle of a beat, to turn one's heart into a handful of dust,"[3] as a source of the line in "The Burial of the Dead": "I will show you fear in a handful of dust."

"The Return" tells of a young English couple, affluent and conventionally happy (as the husband assumes) through five years of a marriage—a marriage which ends abruptly with a seemingly unexpected crisis. On returning home one evening, the husband discovers on his wife's dressing-table a hastily written note: she has gone off with another man, a literary person, editor of a periodical of which the husband has been financial patron. The story recounts in detail the stages of shock, anger, panic, anguish, and confusion experienced by the husband, as he alternates between recalling the past and facing the future. Then the wife returns. She has changed her mind. During their confrontation, the man is revealed as cruel, self-righteous, conventionally pompous and histrionic. Their exchange of words reveals the couple as failing utterly to communicate. Eventually the man falls into a mood of reconciliation, of awakening to the spiritual values of faith and love, of hope that he and his wife can share such a relation, and he reaches to embrace her. But she interprets his gesture as a sexual advance and screams, "This is odious." The husband's awakening becomes one of genuine and final disaffection. He leaves the house. The final words of the story are, "He never returned."

The story is marked by details—especially images—which recur in such a way as to produce an effect of motif and symbol. Prominent among these is the husband's mirror experience in the room where he finds his wife's note. The experience recurs at least seven times throughout the story, producing various effects for the husband as well as for the reader. The first of these mirror scenes is described at some length when the husband enters the room where he will soon find his wife's note:

> The room was empty, of course; but as he stepped in, it became filled all at once with a stir of many people; because the strips of glass on the doors of wardrobes and his wife's large pier-glass reflected him from head to foot, and multiplied his image into a crowd of gentlemanly and slavish imitators, who were dressed exactly like himself; had the same restrained and rare gestures; who moved when he moved, stood still with him in an obsequious immobility, and had just such appearances of life and feeling as he thought it dignified

and safe for any man to manifest. And like real people who are slaves of common thoughts, that are not even their own, they affected a shadowy independence by the superficial variety of their movements. They moved together with him; but they either advanced to meet him, or walked away from him; they appeared, disappeared; they seemed to dodge behind walnut furniture, to be seen again, far within the polished panes, stepping about distinct and unreal in the convincing illusion of a room. And like the men he respected they could be trusted to do nothing individual, original, or startling—nothing unforeseen and nothing improper.[4]

One of Conrad's purposes is, obviously, to characterize the husband, as stated in the final sentence above. But more relevant to my purpose is the similarity of language and imagery to mirror scenes in "Segismund" and *Paradise Lost*. Although "A Game of Chess" does not contain such language and imagery, these are contained in what I have called the ambience of the poem. Because that is actually the case, I recalled "The Return," and on re-reading it discovered correspondences to such an extent that Conrad, because of *Heart of Darkness* plus "The Return," could be considered a major influence on Eliot's poetry. I say "could be" because there are reservations and implications to be considered. And questions to be raised. Is it possible that Conrad is echoing Milton's mirror scene? It would seem unlikely. Yet, a few moments later in the story the husband is described as comparable to the newly fallen Adam of Genesis:

He stood alone, naked and afraid, like the first man on the first day of evil. There are in life events, contacts, glimpses, that seem brutally to bring all the past to a close. There is a shock and a crash, as of a gate flung to behind one by the perfidious hand of fate. Go and seek another paradise, fool or sage. There is a moment of dumb dismay, and the wanderings must begin again; the painful explaining away of facts, the feverish raking up of illusions, the cultivation of a fresh crop of lies in the sweat of one's brow, to sustain life, to make it supportable, to make it fair, so as to hand intact to another generation of blind wanderers the charming legend of a heartless country, of a promised land, all flowers and blessings.... [5]

This passage as quoted concludes a paragraph—and the very next paragraph contains the sentence which speaks of "fear that seems, in the very middle of a beat, to turn one's heart into a handful of dust."

But the fallen Adam allusion, like the mirror scene(s), belongs not to the body of Eliot's sources but to that large ambience which includes the sources. In another manner of speaking, these materials (mirror and Adam) belong to a continuum of associations which Eliot's poetry produces for me, so the continuum may also have existed for Eliot and may have operated in his experience of writing the poetry.

As stated earlier, Robert L. Morris quoted source passages from the final scene of "The Return." There are, however, equally impressive passages very soon after the opening of the story. Most impressive, and much like a passage quoted by Morris, is the description of the husband's arrival home:

> He ascended without footfalls. Brass rods glimmered all up the red carpet. On the first floor landing a marble woman, decently covered from neck to instep with stone draperies, advanced a row of lifeless toes to the edge of the pedestal, and thrust out blindly a rigid white arm holding a cluster of lights.... Heavy curtains caught back, half concealed dark corners. On the rich, stamped paper of the walls hung sketches, water-colours, engravings.[6]

There follows a catalogue of the pictures, vivid and familiar, ending with "large photographs of some famous bas-reliefs...a massacre turned into stone." The very next paragraph contains the first mirror scene, and the succeeding paragraph tells of the husband discovering the wife's note: "he saw appearing at his back, in the high mirror, the corner of his wife's dressing-table, and, amongst the glitter of silver-mounted objects on it, the square white patch of an envelope." There is an obvious correspondence of details with "A Game of Chess": the opulent interior, the subject of footfalls on the stair, the marble, the cluster of lights, the mirror, the pictures on the wall, the glitter of objects on the woman's dressing-table. Another kind of correspondence occurs later in the story, toward the end, in an account of the husband's reflections about his wife: "What did she think?... What did she think during all those years? What did she think yesterday—to-day; what would she think tomorrow?... And he would never know what she meant. Never! Never!"[7] Corresponding to these expressions of the husband's thoughts are these words of the woman in Eliot's poem:

> "What are you thinking of? What thinking? What?
> "I never know what you are thinking. Think."

And also,

> "What shall I do now? What shall I do?"
> ....
> "...What shall we do tomorrow?
> "What shall we ever do?"

A less impressive correspondence between Conrad's man and Eliot's woman is in one of the mirrors scenes, where the man (like Eliot's woman) is brushing his hair:

> He brushed with care, watching the effect of his smoothing; and another face, slightly pale and more tense than was perhaps desirable, peered back at him from the toilet glass. He laid the brushes down, and was not satisfied. He took them up again and brushed, brushed mechanically—forgot himself in that occupation.[8]

If this and other associations seem forced and over-alerted (and they do in some measure), I have chosen to put them on the record because I have on occasions, like other readers, been under-alerted, and those polarities of recognition belong to a subject of some interest and significance.

Besides "A Game of Chess," there are other parts of The Waste Land and there are other poems for which there are correspondences in "The Return"—most strikingly the "handful of dust" already mentioned. That is in "The Burial of the Dead," and there too is the "heap of broken images" which may be associated with Conrad's "mutilated bas-reliefs...a massacre turned into stone." Moving to other poems, I shall first quote from "The Return," so that my associations, eventually stated, may be tested against the reader's associations, if any:

> A chill gust of wind, wandering through the damp and sooty obscurity over the waste of roofs and chimney-pots, touched his face with a clammy flick. He saw an illimitable darkness, in which stood a black jumble of walls, and, between them, the many rows of gaslights stretched far away in long lines, like strung-up beads of fire. A sinister loom as of a hidden conflagration lit up faintly from below the mist, falling upon a billowy and motionless sea of tiles and bricks. At the rattle of the opened window the world seemed to leap out of the night and confront him, while floating up to his ears there came a sound vast and faint; the deep mutter of something immense and alive. It penetrated him with a feeling of dismay and he gasped

silently. From the cab-stand in the square came distinct hoarse voices and a jeering laugh which sounded ominously harsh and cruel.[9]

This description of a London evening has an atmospheric quality like that of Eliot's "Preludes," especially the first Prelude where some specific correspondences are "a gusty shower," "chimney-pots," the "cab-horse" steaming and stamping "at the corner of the street," and "the lighting of the lamps." As at the end of the passage, there is an image of harsh laughter at the end of "Preludes." "Morning at the Window" and the "yellow fog" passage of "Prufrock" share with "Preludes" an imagistic and atmospheric quality like that scene of the damp, sooty, and misty world outside the window of Conrad's story. Another kind of correspondence with the story is in "Hysteria," the short prose-poem of the *Prufrock* group, where a man describes his sense of being physically affected by a woman's hysterical paroxysms:

> As she laughed I was aware of becoming involved in her laughter and being part of it, . . . I was drawn in by short gasps, inhaled at each momentary recovery, lost finally in the dark caverns of her throat, bruised by the ripple of unseen muscles.

In the story the description of the wife's fit of hysteria and its effect upon the man is equally vivid and similar in some details:

> He thought the piercing noise was a delusion. But another shrill peal followed by a deep sob and succeeded by another shriek of mirth positively seemed to tear him out from where he stood. . . . then, as if swept away before another burst of laughter, he disappeared in a flash out of three looking-glasses, vanished suddenly from before her.[10]

This concurrence of hysteria and mirror scene gives emphasis to both, especially as they relate to the continuum of associations within Eliot's poetry and between the poetry and the multifarious sources that are echoed.

Whatever else may be reflected by the "wilderness of mirrors" toward the end of "Gerontion," we can also see in them mirror scenes of "The Return." Some of these have already been quoted, but one more will reflect an emphasis on the aspect of wilderness:

> . . . he looked up, and saw to the left, to the right, in front, men sitting far off in chairs and looking at him with wild eyes—emissaries of a

distracted mankind intruding to spy upon his pain and his humilia-
tion.... He rose quickly, and the others jumped up too on all sides.[11]

In "Portrait of a Lady" the young man whose "self-possession gutters"
when he feels "Like one who smiles, and turning shall remark/
Suddenly, his expression in a glass" is like the husband in "The
Return" on this occasion:

> He caught sight of himself in the pier glass, drawn up to his full
> height, and with a face so white that his eyes, at the distance,
> resembled the black cavities in a skull. He saw himself as if about to
> launch imprecations, with his arms uplifted above her bowed head.
> He was ashamed of that unseemly posture, and put his hands in his
> pockets hurriedly.[12]

My initial concern has been with the "parallels...in image and
tone" between "A Game of Chess," and "The Return," as first indicated
by Robert L. Morris and further documented here. Although it may
already be obvious, it should be added that the similarity of tone is not
just between fifty lines of Eliot's poetry and a few paragraphs of
Conrad's story, for the tone extends beyond each. This is a subject with
several facets. One of these is the similarity of details and thus of
atmosphere—the "image and tone" of the specific passages. Another
is the human situation which prevails throughout "The Return," the
oppressive and distressing failure of communication between a man
and a woman. This is the theme too of "A Game of Chess," and indeed
it is pervasive in Eliot, from "Conversation Galante" through *The
Waste Land* and into the plays. Once we become aware that Eliot was
profoundly and abidingly impressed by this story, we may feel that
correspondences between Eliot and Conrad have a resonance that is
beyond mere coincidence, even if some correspondences are less
striking and substantial than others. There are times when it is not
clear where the resonance begins or ends. To say this, to acknowledge
it, is to add emphasis to the fact that the resonance exists. *The Family
Reunion* provides at least one example of this kind of correspondence,
when the protagonist Harry speaks these words to his cousin Mary:

> One thing you cannot know:
> The sudden extinction of every alternative,
> The unexpected crash of the iron cataract.
> You do not know what hope is, until you have lost it.[13]

In relation with this we may recall Conrad's analogy of the husband with the fallen Adam: "He stood alone, naked and afraid, like the first man on the first day of evil. There are in life events, contacts, glimpses, that seem brutally to bring all the past to a close. There is a shock and a crash, as of a gate flung to behind one by the perfidious hand of fate."[14] Later in the story there is this comparable passage: "With a short thrill he saw himself an exiled, forlorn figure in a realm of ungovernable, of unrestrained folly. Nothing could be foreseen, foretold—guarded against. And the sensation was intolerable, had something of the withering horror that may be conceived as following upon the utter extinction of all hope."[15] If there is coincidence here, it is not just coincidence of crash and extinction, but also of the immediate contexts, and also of the larger contexts, Conrad's story and Eliot's play, both of them vivid representations of intensities of alienation between men and women, husbands and wives, which are also the intensities that are represented in "A Game of Chess."

In my earlier essay on Conrad and Eliot I dwelt at length on the detailed and pervasive influence of Conrad's *Heart of Darkness* on Eliot's poems and plays. Because of statements which he has made on the subject, I assume that B. C. Southam found that essay convincing: "Next to Dante, Conrad's story is arguably the most important single literary experience in Eliot's poetry from 'Prufrock' onwards." And also: "Conrad's nightmare vision would have made sense to Dante; and one would judge that these two writers were felt by Eliot to exert a single force flowing into and impowering his imagination."[16] If we agree, we might want to urge that "The Return" should be added to *Heart of Darkness* as part of a special "literary experience" and "force." But for all my sympathy with Southam's emphasis, I can no longer agree that any two literary experiences, let alone any two writers, have been the most important and most forceful influences on Eliot's poetry. But that the influences, however many, are a single force—that is an appealing idea. It was, after all, the mirror scenes of "Segismund" and of *Paradise Lost* which led me to Conrad's "The Return."

VI
"Other Echoes..."

"The Hidden Stream"

There is reason to turn again to Benson's magniloquent comment on FitzGerald's most famous work:

> Omar does not go to the wine-jar only that he may forget, but that he may also remember. He feeds on honey-dew and drinks the milk of paradise that he may banish for a little the terror of the unknown, the bewildered mystery of life, the pain, the shame, the fear, and the dark shadow that nearer or further lies across the road; thus much to forget; and then he is perchance, enabled to remember the sweet days, the spring and the budding rose; to remember that though the beginning and the end are dark, yet that the God of Pain and Death is also the maker of the fair world, the gracious charm of voice and hand, the woven tapestry of tree and meadow-grass, the sunset burning red behind the dark tree-trunks of the grove, the voice of music, the song of the bird, the whisper of leaves, the murmur of the hidden stream—of all the sights and sounds that fill the heart full and leave it yearning, unsatisfied with the pain that is itself a joy.

I have quoted again this passage from Benson's peroration to his chapter on FitzGerald's masterpiece because I wish to compare it with a passage from the peroration of his book on Walter Pater. (The books *Edward FitzGerald* and *Walter Pater*, both in the English Men of Letters series, were published respectively in 1905 and 1906). My reason for quoting this passage will be apparent enough:

> There is a spell unknown to those who live the eager life of affairs, who dwell in crowded cities, or who carry the busy scheming mind abroad with them into lonelier places; the spell that broods over the wooded valley with its hazel-hidden stream, where the bird sings among the thickets; the spell that lies behind the dark tree-trunks of the grove that bar the smouldering sunset with shafts of shade; that trembles in the green twilight when the stars begin to glimmer, and the winds are hushed.[1]

Conspicuous here are details identical with those in Benson's Omar passage. At one point there is the word for word repetition, "behind the dark tree-trunks of the grove," in each case related to the same image, "the sunset burning" in the first passage and "the smouldering sunset" in the second. Conspicuous also are the repeated references to the song of the bird and the hidden stream. The two passages, especially in the parts that are so similar, occur on similar occasions in each book and are unmistakably calculated to produce the same meaning and the same effect. Benson could be accused of serving up the same ready-made rhetorical recipe, and in one sense this is true. But I am persuaded that the repetitions are evidence of Benson's own genuine sensibility and abiding intensities, which were summoned to expression when he contemplated personalities, FitzGerald and Pater, for whom he had a special affinity. Benson's repetition in Pater of what he had written in FitzGerald may be regarded as evidence of the charge of meaning which those phrases and images had for Benson, and to which Eliot responded—those are pearls that were his eyes, as Eliot recalled with reference to the images of "Kubla Khan" and its origins in Coleridge's reading.[2] In the same context[3] Eliot informs us that he borrowed the same imagery twice from Chapman, who in turn had borrowed it from Seneca, although he does not say whether he was aware of this at the time of borrowing or became aware of it afterward. This kind of echoing from one writer to another I have already indicated, and I find such a chain of echoes again in the passages quoted from Benson's books. Obviously enough, Benson is echoing himself. But in the first instance (and hence in both) he is echoing Paradise Lost—in fact, the descriptions of Eden in Book IV to which we attended in connection with "Segismund" and "A Game of Chess." Benson's catalogues of the beautiful particulars of nature are Edenic—moreover, Edenic according to Milton. It is precisely those details in Benson's passage on Omar and the wine-jar which have correspondences, on the one hand, in Eliot's poetry, and on the other, in Book IV, as in these familiar lines:

> murmuring waters fall
> Down the slope hills, dispersed, or in a lake
> That to the fringed bank with myrtle crowned,
> Her crystal mirror holds, unite their streams.
> The birds their choir apply; airs, vernal airs,
> Breathing the smell of field and grove, attune
> The trembling leaves,...
>
> (ll. 260–266)

In this one passage we find details that match Benson: "the grove, the voice of music, the song of the bird, the whisper of leaves, the murmur of the hidden stream.... " Additional correspondences occur in the immediate context of Book IV. For Benson's "sunset burning red behind the dark tree-trunks of the grove" there are these: "the unpierced shade/Embrowned the noontide bow'rs" (ll. 245–6); "Groves whose rich trees wept odorous gums and balm" (l. 248); "that sweet grove/Of Daphne by Orontes" (ll. 272–3). For Benson's "whispers of leaves": "gentle gales/ ... whisper whence they stole/Those balmy spoils" (ll. 156, 157–8); "a tuft of shade that on a green/Stood whispering soft" (ll. 325–6). For Benson's "murmur of the hidden stream" (with emphasis on "murmur" and "hidden"): "a murmuring sound/Of waters issued from a cave" (ll. 453–4).

It could be justifiably argued that Benson's passages in *FitzGerald* and *Pater* are nature-rhetoric typical of the nineteenth and early twentieth centuries. But it could just as well be claimed that both Benson and Milton partake of archetypes of landscape, ideal and idealized, which go back to biblical and classical traditions. To recognize such continuities does not preclude recognizing also Eliot's specific continuities with Benson and Milton, especially since there is otherwise a pattern of correspondence. The already existing pattern justifies new recognitions, and new recognitions enlarge and reinforce the pattern.

One aspect of the pattern is the fact that in his echoings Eliot frequently participates in an already established momentum of echoings—or he echoes what is already resonant. As do others. For example, in the passage that has been under consideration Benson says of Omar, "He feeds on honey-dew and drinks the milk of paradise," quite openly, if approximately, quoting the famous ending of Coleridge's "Kubla Khan," where Coleridge, of course, is echoing the biblical image of a paradise regained, a land flowing with milk and honey. Coleridge's poem has long been famous for a number of reasons, including the fact that it has been, since John Livingston Lowes' *The Road to Xanadu*, the example *par excellence* of multiple echoes from a poet's reading. It has become a commonplace observation that Coleridge's "Abyssinian maid/... Singing of Mount Abora" derives from Book IV of *Paradise Lost*: "where Abassin kings their issue guard,/Mount Amara..." (ll. 280–81). The similarity is not just that of proper names but of several details in the terrains of Coleridge's Xanadu and Milton's Eden, such as Xanadu's "gardens bright with sinuous rills,/Where blossomed many an incense-bearing tree" and

Eden's "Groves whose rich trees wept odorous gums and balm" (l. 248). Xanadu's sacred river "meandering with a mazy motion/ Through wood and dale" and Eden's brooks rolling "With mazy error under pendant shades" (l. 239). This Xanadu-Eden relationship is complicated by the fact that Milton and Coleridge were both retentive readers of Samuel Purchas, and in this case specifically of the chapter "Of the Hill Amara" in *Purchas, His Pilgrimage*.[4] There is thus a line of echoing from Purchas to Milton and then from Purchas and Milton to Coleridge. In this case the line does not continue to Eliot—at least, I find no direct line to Eliot from "Kubla Khan." For many years, however, I have felt an affinity between that poem and certain parts of Eliot's poetry, specifically poems and passages where the imagery contributes to an effect of lyrical intensity and a personal immediacy of expression. I am therefore impressed with some statements made by C. K. Stead in his comments on *The Waste Land*: "Parts of the poem stand (this is not a question of 'evaluation') with a few other poems ('Kubla Khan' is another example) as the purest 'poetry' in the language, the irreducible 'first voice.' It is not a vehicle or an agent, but a self-contained poetic entity." And further: "If one contemplates 'The Waste Land' long enough it can seem the most uncompromising poetry ever written in English, wrung, like 'Kubla Khan,' from a mind so confident in abstract discourse, so capable of 'explaining' itself, that the procession of non-discursive images could only have been achieved by a discipline amounting to self-annihilation. What opium or some rarely attained dream state precipitated in Coleridge in 1797 (*pace* Miss Elisabeth Schneider), a 'breakdown' precipitated more thoroughly in Eliot in the winter of 1921."[5] An intriguing and curious matter here is the fact that Stead twice mentions "Kubla Khan" as a prime example of the purest poetry, the irreducible first voice, a procession of non-discursive images precipitated by a rare and highly subjective experience—yet without also mentioning (what Stead surely knows) that Coleridge's poem is in large part echoed from Milton and other sources. Stead's emphasis on the analogy with "Kubla Khan" accords with my observation that in Eliot's poetry the effects of lyrical intensity and personal immediacy are often produced by passages (especially non-discursive images) which are echoes (and precipitations) out of Eliot's own reading.

It will be recalled that Benson's Edenic passage on Omar reaches back to "Kubla Khan" and Book IV of *Paradise Lost*, and that it reaches ahead to *Four Quartets* and Eliot's early plays. Coleridge's poem is otherwise relevant in that it is a conspicuous example of the kind of complex and compounded echoings which are found in Eliot's poems. It will also be recalled that Book IV, which figures among the Miltonic elements present in *Four Quartets,* is a major presence in the network of associations which is both intimated and indicated by "A Game of Chess." Milton's presence in Eliot's poetry is therefore substantial, but for my awareness of how substantial that presence is, I am indebted to Benson's quotation of "Segismund" and to his comment on Omar—which are also presences in Eliot's poetry.[6]

While the eloquent passages in Benson's *FitzGerald* and *Pater* are so similar (even identical) at certain points, it is the rhythmic catalogue of images in *FitzGerald* which produces recognition of a relation with Eliot. It is not unlikely that Eliot had read *Pater,* but there is no evidence that he had. In describing Pater's rooms at Oxford, Benson reminds us of *Burnt Norton* with the statement, "His only luxury was a bowl of dried rose-leaves."[7] But Eliot must have encountered other bowls of rose-leaves.

"Now, Now, the Bird is on the Wing"

"I find it strange that none of the numerous commentators on Eliot's work (as far as I know) have noticed the similarity in conception between *Burnt Norton* ... and Lawrence's essay, since both deal with an identical theme, the 'moment.'" So stated Giorgio Melchiori in "The Lotus and the Rose," a chapter of his *The Tightrope Walkers.*[8] The essay to which Melchiori referred is the Preface which D. H. Lawrence wrote for the American edition of his *New Poems* (1920) and which was reprinted in the posthumous collection *Phoenix* in 1936. This is the same year, as Melchiori observed, that *Burnt Norton* was first printed, so that to know the essay, it is likely that Eliot had read the original Preface. It is a justification and celebration of free verse and is itself a kind of prose poem. Melchiori points out not only "similarity in conception" but numerous echoes of language, imagery and idea in *Four Quartets,* and especially in *Burnt Norton.* It is both strange and not strange that Lawrence's essay, and Melchiori's chapter as well, have gone unnoticed, since so much else has gone (and may still go) unnoticed and unrecognized. Anyone interested in Eliot's poetry, and in the general subject of literary influence, should read Melchiori's chapter, and Lawrence's short essay (about two thousand words).[9]

As Melchiori observes, *Burnt Norton* echoes a cluster of details which are themselves rhapsodically repeated in Lawrence's essay, all of them related to the central idea of the "moment." But Lawrence's moment and Eliot's moment, so much alike, are yet essentially different. Eliot's moment—in the rose garden, in the arbour where the rain beat, in the draughty church at smokefall—is the moment out of time, the moment in which time is conquered. Lawrence's moment is the moment of *carpe diem*, seize-the-day concentrated to an ecstatic and awesome awareness of existence and sensation in the immediate present, the moment in time and of time which he proclaims is rendered by free verse:

> Such is the rare new poetry. One realm we have never conquered: the pure present. One great mystery of time is *terra incognita* to us: the instant. The most superb mystery we have hardly recognized: the immediate, instant self. The quick of all time is the instant. The quick of all the universe, of all creation, is the incarnate, carnal self.

These statements are immediately preceded by the following:

> The bird is on the wing in the winds, flexible to every breath, a living spark in the storm, its very flickering depending upon its supreme mutability and power of change. Whence such a bird came: whither it goes: from what solid earth it will close its wings and settle, this is not the question. This is a question of before and after. Now, *now*, the bird is on the wing in the winds.[10]

"The Bird of Time has but a little way/To flutter—and the Bird is on the Wing": FitzGerald's *Omar*. Lawrence has revised *Omar* as well as echoed, changing the sense to *but the bird is on the wing—Now, now*.

"Quick, said the bird.... " "Quick now, here, now, always—/ Ridiculous the waste sad time/Stretching before and after." The dash between "always" and "Ridiculous" separates the voice of the poet from the voice of the bird, Lawrence's bird appropriated from *Omar* and from Shelley's Skylark ("We look before and after,/And pine for what is not"), Eliot's bird appropriated from various sources, including Lawrence, Shelley, *Omar*. Lawrence's essay abounds with the motifs which are the motifs of *Burnt Norton* (and of *Four Quartets*): the quick (I counted eleven); the Now (capitalized); before and after; past, present and future; beginning and end. Some of these and their equivalents are present in every one of Lawrence's short paragraphs. Present also are symbolic images which are also the symbolic images, such as the lotus and rose, of Eliot's poem—as in this entire paragraph:

> Life, the everpresent, knows no finality, no finished crystallisation. The perfect *rose* is only a running *flame*, emerging and flowing off, and never in any sense at rest, static, finished. Herein lies its

transcendent loveliness. The whole tide of all life and all time suddenly *heaves*, and appears before us as *an apparition, a revelation*. We look at the very *white quick* of nascent creation. A *water-lily heaves* herself from the flood, looks around, gleams and is gone. We have seen the incarnation, *the quick* of the ever-swirling flood. We have seen the invisible. We have seen, we have touched, we have partaken of the very substance of creative change, creative mutation. If you tell me about *the lotus*, tell me of nothing changeless or eternal. Tell me of the mystery of the inexhaustible, forever-unfolding creative spark. Tell me of the incarnate disclosure of the *flux*, mutation in blossom, laughter and decay perfectly open in their *transit*, nude in their *movement*, before us. [italics added][11]

Much of this is matched in *Burnt Norton*—and the rose-flame corresponds with "the fire and the rose are one," the final words of *Little Gidding* and of the final strophe, which in one aspect is a catalogue of the major motifs of *Four Quartets* and especially of *Burnt Norton*. Farther along in Lawrence's paragraph there is the apparition, the white quick, the lotus which heaves from the water, gleams and is gone—all of this so close to

> the pool was filled with water out of sunlight,
> And the lotos rose, quietly, quietly,
> The surface glittered out of heart of light,

and close also to

> a grace of sense, a white light still and moving,
> *Erhebung* without motion, concentration
> Without elimination,...

In Lawrence's paragraph, the lotus is apposite to "the very white quick of nascent creation," and Eliot's *Erhebung* is apposite to "a white light," while all of these are in a continuum of apposition, of correspondence. I have made this observation in order to speculate that Eliot's use of the German word owes something to Lawrence's twice-repeated "heaves." In German, *Erhebung* is used in mystical contexts to mean rapture, uplift, elevation. Its root element is *heben*, etymologically the same word as *heave*, both words meaning, to lift or raise.

I have added the emphasis to *flux, transit,* and *movement* in Lawrence's paragraph because these are words and ideas of major significance in *Burnt Norton*, and also because near the end of his essay

Lawrence concentrates these meanings into the repeated statement, "the bird is on the wing," for the bird has travelled from FitzGerald's quatrain to Lawrence's paragraph to Eliot's poem.

VII
"...Inhabit the Garden"

FitzGerald's *Rubáiyát of Omar Khayyám*, Benson's feelingful comment on it, the "Segismund" speech—these have been my main subjects in relation to Eliot's poetry. Each of these, as we have seen, has a relation to the well-known rose-garden theme, for even "Segismund" has garden imagery as well as other links with the Garden of Eden as described in Book IV of *Paradise Lost*. In my essay on *Ash Wednesday* (1939) I first called attention to this theme of a childhood experience in a rose-garden, an experience of which the quality and meaning are both sexual and religious. In another essay (1942) I explored at length this theme as it is expressed and developed in the poetry and plays which Eliot had written up to that time—that is, up to *Burnt Norton* and *The Family Reunion*, and it is in these that the rose-garden experience is most striking and is expressed most fully.[1] In the latter essay I was concerned with what I called "a persistent theme" and an "aspect of continuity" in Eliot's poetry. I did not consider possible echoes and sources except, at the opening of the essay, to present the subject by quoting at length Eliot's comment on the sexual experience in childhood as described by Dante in the *Vita Nuova*. It was therefore with much interest and some chagrin that I first encountered "sources" for Eliot's rose-garden in an essay by Louis L. Martz (1947).[2] Since then, other sources have been claimed. Because I propose to offer a source that is presumably "new," I shall first review some that have already been offered.

One of the sources to which Martz referred is *Alice in Wonderland*. In the first chapter, after falling down the rabbit-hole and arriving in a long, low hall, Alice found on a little glass table a tiny golden key which fitted a little door that was behind a curtain:

> Alice opened the door and found that it led into a small passage, not much larger than a rat-hole: she knelt down and looked along the passage into the loveliest garden you ever saw. How she longed to get out of that dark hall, and wander about among those beds of bright flowers and those cool fountains, but she could not even get her head through the doorway.[3]

Alice remembered the lovely garden throughout several adventures and finally, after eating a mushroom at the Mad Tea-Party, she shrinks to the right size: "then she walked down the little passage: and *then*—she found herself at last in the beautiful garden, among the bright flower-beds and the cool fountains."[4] Martz's other source is D. H. Lawrence's short story "The Shadow in the Rose Garden": the story tells of a husband and wife who are vacationing at a resort community where, prior to their marriage, the wife was employed for two years. During this period the wife had had a love affair with a man who, she believes, subsequently died in the war. That is her reason for being drawn back to this scene of her past, but the husband is not aware of any of this. Lawrence describes the experience of the woman as she revisits a rose-garden which belongs to her nostalgic memory of that early love:

> Slowly she went down one path, lingering, like one who has gone back into the past.... So, slowly, like a white, pathetic butterfly, she drifted down the path, coming at last to a tiny terrace all full of roses. They seemed to fill the place, a sunny, gay throng. She was shy of them, they were so many and so bright. They seemed to be conversing and laughing. She felt herself in a strange crowd. It exhilarated her, carried her out of herself.

She took a seat among the roses, and in another moment "she started cruelly as a shadow crossed her and a figure moved into her sight."[5] A man has approached her whom she recognizes as the lover who she thought was killed—whom she very soon observes to be insane, "a lunatic." *Alice* and Lawrence's story have a special authority as sources of the garden imagery in *Burnt Norton* and *The Family Reunion*. Martz reports that "Mr. Eliot has remarked in conversation upon the importance of *Alice in Wonderland* here."[6] Eliot had dwelt at some length and with some praise on Lawrence's story in *After Strange Gods*. On reading Martz's essay, I was reminded of the gardens in *Alice* and in Lawrence, but I failed to recall them earlier, while writing my essay on the rose-garden, because at that time I was under-alerted for sources. Martz apparently was unaware of, or unmindful of, the Lawrence essay on free verse which Melchiori was to recognize as a substantial part of the Lawrentian source for a pattern of symbolic images in *Burnt Norton*.

A very tentative consideration of source was made by Helen Gardner (in *The Art of T. S. Eliot*, 1950) in a statement so brief that I shall quote it entire: "It has been suggested to me that the setting of the poem [*Burnt Norton*] and the image of the laughing hidden children may have been caught from Rudyard Kipling's story 'They.' The children in that story are both 'what might have been and what has been,' appearing to those who have lost their children in the house of a blind woman who has never borne a child."[7] Gardner means that children are seen and/or heard in the house and on its grounds only by persons who have lost a child through death or who, like the blind mistress of the estate, have never borne a child. The story is told by a first-person narrator. Motoring in a remote part of England, he arrived at an ancient house and had (very near the opening of the story) this experience:

> A child appeared at an upper window, and I thought the little thing waved a friendly hand. But it was to call a companion, for presently another bright head showed. Then I heard a laugh among the yew-peacocks, and turning to make sure (till then I had been watching the house only) I saw the silver fountain behind a hedge thrown up against the sun. The doves on the roof cooed to the cooing water; but between the two notes I caught the utterly happy chuckle of a child absorbed in some light mischief.

Then the blind mistress of the house came through the garden door, and in conversation with the narrator soon remarked, "We're so out of the world here."[8] There are apparent correspondences between these details and Eliot's imagery of children laughing in the garden. An effect of the story is the reader's growing awareness that the narrator, like some staff-members of the household, sees and hears these children because he too is the bereaved parent of a dead child.

In her book on Eliot, Elisabeth Schneider says that she finds the "main origin" of the rose-garden imagery in Oscar Wilde's fairy tale "The Selfish Giant." As compared to Kipling's story, she says, "the spirit and the imagery of Wilde's story are closer to those of Eliot."[9] The story opens with an account of children playing in a garden where there are blossoming peach trees and singing birds. The owner of the garden is a giant who, on returning from a sojourn of seven years, frightens the children from the garden, builds a high wall around it and puts up the sign "Trespassers Will Be Prosecuted." As a result the garden remains locked in winter snow and frost the year round, to the giant's dismay. Then one morning he wakens to find the garden filled with singing birds, fragrant flowers, blossoming trees and playing children:

> He saw a most wonderful sight. Through a little hole in the wall the children had crept in, and they were sitting in the branches of the trees. In every tree that he could see there was a little child. And the trees were so glad to have the children back again that they had covered themselves with blossoms, and were waving their arms gently above the children's heads. The birds were flying about and twittering with delight, and the flowers were looking up through the green grass and laughing.[10]

In a corner of the garden, however, one tree is still barren and wintry, and beneath it there is a small boy too little to climb the tree. When the giant sees this, he goes to the boy and reaches him into the tree, which then breaks into blossom. That same tree blossoms again one winter morning, when the giant has grown old and frail. On noticing the tree, he goes to it and finds the same little boy, with nail wounds, the stigmata, on hands and feet. He says to the giant, "you shall come with me to my garden, which is Paradise," and the story ends with the image of the giant "lying dead under the tree, all covered with white blossoms."

Impressive as Wilde's story and Schneider's claims for it may be, it turns out that Gardner's modest claim for Kipling's story was sound enough—in fact, confirmed by a letter from Eliot to John Hayward, 5 August 1941, as reported by Gardner in her book *The Composition of Four Quartets* (1978). Having quoted the relevant parts of Eliot's letter, Gardner observes that Eliot recognized sources of *Burnt Norton* in Kipling's story and in Elizabeth Barrett Browning's poem "The Lost Bower," of which the four opening lines are quoted in the story. Gardner suggests that Eliot knew the entire long poem and goes on to say, "I think unconsciously it contributed more than Kipling's story to *Burnt Norton*."[11] But neither the poem nor the story is especially striking as a source of *Burnt Norton*—a fact which justifies the consideration that other texts may also have served Eliot as sources of the poem, that here as elsewhere a single locus of the poetry may combine and merge several sources.

Yet another possible source is H. G. Wells' short story "The Door in the Wall"—never before claimed as such, to my knowledge.[12] Much of the story is the recounting by a first-person narrator of what a life-long friend, Lionel Wallace, had told him at dinner, a dream-like matter. The friend had told "of the thing that was hidden in his life, the haunting memory of a beauty and a happiness that filled his heart with insatiable longings, that made all the interests and spectacle of

worldly life seem dull and tedious and vain to him."[13] This hidden
thing was a green door in a white wall on a street otherwise filled with
"mean dirty shops." Wallace recalled that as a child about five years
and four months old, in the month of October, finding himself in front
of the door, he overcame all fears and restraints, abruptly entering the
door, and "came into the garden that has haunted all his life...."

> There was something in the very air of it that exhilarated, that gave
> one a sense of lightness and good happening and well being; there
> was something in the sight of it that made all its colour clean and
> perfect and subtly luminous. In the instant of coming into it one was
> exquisitely glad—as only in rare moments, and when one is young
> and joyful and one can be glad in this world. And everything was
> beautiful there....

Wallace described in detail what he saw and experienced and felt:

> It was ... an enchanted garden.... And somehow it was just like
> coming home.... I became in a moment a very glad and wonder-
> happy little boy—in another world. It was a world with a different
> quality, a warmer, more penetrating and mellower light, with a faint
> clear gladness in its air, and wisps of sun-touched cloud in the
> blueness of its sky.

In this enchanted garden Wallace petted two tame panthers, was
kissed by a tall, fair girl, played delightful games with playmates. But
soon a sombre woman led him away and showed him a book that was
the story of his own life, the pages not just pictures but realities, so
that his contemplation of the book delivered him "outside the green
door in the long white wall."[14] Throughout the course of a successful
life as student and statesman, Wallace encountered the green door a
number of times, but each time he declined to enter—because he
should not be late at school, because he was eager to keep a first
rendezvous with a woman he loved, because he was hastening to his
father's death-bed, because of the pressure of political circumstances.
Finally, as a middle-aged man, Wallace turned desperately to looking
for the green door, as he explained to the narrator: "My soul is full of
inappeasable regrets. At nights—when it is less likely I shall be
recognized—I go out. I wander.... A Cabinet Minister, ... wandering
alone —grieving—sometimes near audibly lamenting—for a door, for
a garden!" Toward the end of the story the narrator reports that Wallace's body was found "early yesterday morning in a deep excavation"

by which a railway was being extended. Wallace had evidently gone through the small doorway that had been cut in the temporary fencing, the doorway having been left unfastened through a misunderstanding between two workmen. The story ends with the narrator's reflections on Wallace:

> My mind is darkened with questions and riddles. ... Was there, after all, ever any green door in the wall at all? ... I am more than half convinced that he had, in truth, an abnormal gift, and a sense, something—I know not what—that in the guise of a wall and door offered him an outlet, a secret and peculiar passage of escape into another and altogether more beautiful world.[15]

Wells' story, more than those of Lewis Carroll, Kipling, Lawrence, or Wilde, has an immediate correspondence with the garden of Eliot's poetry—and mainly *Burnt Norton*. Like Wells's story, Eliot's poem renders adult memory of a childhood garden-experience. Wells' "secret and peculiar passage of escape into another and altogether more beautiful world" does indeed echo in the mind as we recall Eliot's "passage which we did not take/Towards the door we never opened/Into the rose-garden." The quest for the long-lost playmates behind the green door is like the quest concentrated in these phrases: "find them, find them,/Round the corner. Through the first gate,/Into our first world.... "

In his essay on Dante (1929), commenting on the *Vita Nuova*, Eliot dwelt specifically on the childhood experience as recollected by the adult:

> The type of sexual experience which Dante describes as occurring to him at the age of nine years is by no means impossible or unique.... I cannot find it incredible that what has happened to others should have happened to Dante with much greater intensity.... It is not, I believe, meant as a description of what he *consciously* felt on his meeting with Beatrice, but rather as a description of what that meant on mature reflection upon it.[16]

These and other comments by Eliot on the *Vita Nuova*, as well as the passages of rose-garden and similar imagery in the poems and plays, suggest that Eliot recalled some childhood experience of his own. John Hayward states that this was so in his notes to the French translation of *Four Quartets*.[17] Citing Hayward on this subject, Elisabeth Schneider offers some qualifications of this opinion:

As they appear in the poems, however, the images seem to me rather the grown-up's view of the child's world, not a recovered sense of what that world felt like to the child.... It is not so much the pleasure and excitement experienced by the children, as it is our own pleasure in hearing their excited laughter.... If the children, apple-blossoms, birds, laughter are memory at all, they seem memory heavily overlaid by another's imagination, probably Wilde's, from which they take their character and significance....[18]

By "probably" Schneider appears to mean probably Wilde rather than Kipling. But this leaves out of account the sources in Carroll, Lawrence, and Wells, which have their own claims and claimants, and by which the problem (if it is a problem) thickens. Or we could say that the subject is enriched.

There is, in fact, further evidence on the side of an actual childhood experience—in the lecture Eliot gave in 1959 at the centennial of Mary Institute in St. Louis. This was a school for girls which the poet's grandfather, William Greenleaf Eliot, had founded and named after his own daughter. The Eliot home and the school were immediate neighbors, so that as a boy Eliot watched the girls playing in the school yard, which evidently was a garden in some respects. When the school-day was over and the girls had left, Eliot was permitted to go through a gate into the yard. In the lecture, as reported by the St. Louis *Post-Dispatch*, Eliot recalled one such occasion when something unusual happened: "Once I entered the school yard before the last girls had left. When I looked in a school window and saw a girl looking out at me, I fled out of there in a hurry."[19] Walter J. Ong has said that Eliot's memories of the school yard and the girls may have been the "historical germ" of passages in *Burnt Norton*, that "it is hard to believe that the youthful situation here had nothing whatsoever to do with the poetic actuality." Dennis Donoghue was similarly impressed, remarking that "the playground acquired a strange resonance for him, being a place of young girls, echoes, presences, and absences"—and also, "I am ready to believe that both gardens played some part in the imaginative process which led to the composition,"[20] the other garden being that of Burnt Norton, the mansion in Gloucestershire whose ruins Eliot visited in the summer of 1934 and whose name he took for the title of his poem (presumably thus indicating a personal relevance). Ong and Donoghue are obviously intrigued by the idea that the poet's childhood experience is a source of the poem, but neither Ong nor Donoghue considers that the poetry may reflect an early personal experience that has an accretion of later reading experience, let alone that the personal memory (if any) is "heavily overlaid by another's imagination," as Schneider proposed. So what can be concluded about the matter of sources in this case, if anything? At least this much: that where there is an abundance of possible sources, determination that one has stronger claims than another, or requires greater emphasis than another, is not a matter that can be readily resolved.

An after-thought comes appropriately to mind here. In the After-Notes to my essay dealing with Eliot and Conrad I quote the opening paragraphs of Conrad's short novel *The Shadow-Line,* and I quote them again for a relevance which is self-evident:

> Only the young have such moments. I don't mean the very young. No. The very young have, properly speaking, no moments. It is the privilege of early youth to live in advance of its days in all the beautiful continuity of hope which knows no pauses and no intro-spection.
>
> One closes behind one the little gate of mere boyishness—and enters an enchanted garden. Its very shades glow with promise. Every turn of the path has its seduction. And it isn't because it is an undiscovered country. One knows well enough that all mankind had streamed that way. It is the charm of universal experience from which one expects an uncommon or personal sensation—a bit of one's own.
>
> One goes on recognising the landmarks of the predecessors, excited, amused, taking the hard luck and the good luck together—the kicks and the halfpence, as the saying is—the picturesque common lot that holds so many possibilities for the deserving or perhaps for the lucky. Yes. One goes on. And the time, too, goes on—till one perceives ahead a shadow-line warning one that the region of early youth, too, must be left behind.
>
> This is the period of life in which such moments of which I have spoken are likely to come. What moments? Why, the moments of boredom, of weariness, of dissatisfaction. Rash moments. I mean moments when the still young are inclined to commit rash actions, such as getting married suddenly or else throwing up a job for no reason.[21]

I have quoted quite so much in order to include, first, the image of the "shadow-line," and then, for whatever it may tell if anything, "rash actions, such as getting married suddenly."

VIII
Another Garden

A single main source for the recurring and highly charged rose-garden imagery in Eliot's poetry cannot be readily determined because we cannot be sure that we already know all the eligible sources. For example, there is the juvenile novel *The Secret Garden* by Frances Hodgson Burnett, first published in 1911 and something of a classic in its kind. It is certain that Eliot had read some of the "sources" considered, and wholly plausible that he had read the others. But how likely is it that he had read a juvenile novel which was first published when he was already a young man in his twenties? No telling. The correspondences with Eliot's poetry may be no more than a striking body of coincidence. But the title of the novel is already a correspondence with a singular motif and Eliot, coming across it, might have been drawn to reading the novel—as I was recently drawn to reading *The Secret Garden* (with a vague sensation of re-reading).

The main characters of the novel are a girl and two boys. After the girl's parents have died in a cholera epidemic in India, the sickly and unattractive Mary Lennox is sent to Yorkshire to live in Misselthwaite Manor, the home of her maternal uncle, Archibald Craven, hunchback and affluent widower who is usually travelling abroad. Soon after arriving, Mary learns that on the grounds of the manor there are several gardens, one of which has been untended behind its walls since her uncle's wife died ten years ago. It had been her special garden and after her sudden death, Craven forbade anyone to enter, locking the door to the garden and burying the key. The wife had died in child-birth, soon after an accident: she fell to the ground when a tree-branch on which she had been sitting suddenly broke, at a time when the young couple were visiting in that garden. The story develops as Mary Lennox pursues her curiosity about things at the manor. She hears someone crying at the end of a corridor, and discovers that it is her invalid cousin, Colin Craven, the child at whose birth her uncle's wife had died. The other boy in the story is Dickon Sowerby, younger brother of one of the servant girls. Mary enlists his help in restoring the garden, which she had secretly entered after a friendly robin had led her first to the key and then to the locked, vine-covered door. Mary's delight in the enterprise of restoring the garden with Dickon's knowledgeable help, and her active gardening out in the air and sunshine work a marvellous improvement in her health, temperament and appearance. This secret activity is eventually shared with Colin, whom they have brought to the garden in a wheelchair, and he too is brought to physical and mental health by work and pleasure in the garden. At this point Archibald Craven is summoned home from abroad, and the story ends with the recognition scene of father and son, healthy, happy, and reconciled to life.

Even in this synopsis of the novel some correspondences with Eliot are obvious, whether or not they should be regarded as coincidental. Obvious, of course, are the garden, the bird, the children—all in close relation. The prominence in the novel of the bird may be noted by the fact that one of the chapters is called "The Robin Who Showed the Way," for the bird leads Mary to the key and the door and thus into the garden. Although Schneider had other things in mind with her chapter heading "The Pattern Is Ironed into the Carpet," the idea is applicable to the emphasis with which garden and bird are fitted into the thematic pattern in Eliot's play The Confidential Clerk. In an early moment of the play Eggerson says of Colby: "He's expressed such an interest in my garden/That I think he ought to have window boxes./ Some day he'll want a garden of his own. And yes, a bird bath!"[1] In the novel, while talking to the Craven gardener, Mary asks, "Have you a garden of your own?" And then she soon says, "I—I want to play that—that I have a garden of my own."[2] Such expression is commonplace enough and could be mere coincidence. Yet we know that as coincidences accumulate, they begin to beg the question, so that the possibility of actual echoing arises. That is one reason why I have opened the "case" for The Secret Garden with references to Eliot's play; another reason is the strong coincidence that comes in an exchange of dialogue between Colby and Lucasta. When she says, "You have your secret garden. To which you can retire/And lock the gate behind you"—he replies, "And lock the gate behind me?/Are you sure that you haven't your own secret garden/Somewhere, if you could find it?" In just another moment Colby says, "I turn the key, and walk through the gate,/And there I am...alone, in my 'garden.'"[3] Secret, lock, key, gate—all this is very close to the garden of Frances Hodgson Burnett's novel, and to other gardens as well. Commenting within the novel on Mary and the garden, Burnett says, "The few books she had read and liked had been fairy-story books, and she had read of secret gardens in some of the stories."[4] Yet, among the other gardens which figure as sources, only Carroll's has lock and key, only Wells' is of a secret nature, and in none does a bird figure so prominently.

Another kind of correspondence with the novel is found in the imagery of plant-life affected by the change from winter to spring. In an early chapter the gardener, speaking his Yorkshire dialect, tells Mary of the "good rich earth": "It's *dull* in th' winter when it's got nowt to do. In th' flower gardens out there things will be *stirrin'* down below *in* th' *dark.*" Then Mary soon asks, "Are things *stirring* down below *in the dark* in that garden where he lives?"—referring to the bird and the locked-up garden. In a later chapter Colin, no longer an invalid, chants, "That is the Magic. The flowers are growing—the *roots* are *stirring.* That is the Magic."[5] I have added emphasis to the words which readily recall the famous first lines of *The Waste Land,* and especially "stirring/Dull roots with spring rain." Comparable also but less familiar are words spoken by another Mary, Harry's cousin, in *The Family Reunion*: "The cold spring now is the time/For the ache in the moving root/The agony in the dark."[6] These words are spoken in that exchange of dialogue between Harry and Mary which prefigures the rose-garden dialogue that occurs later in the play between Harry and his aunt Agatha, and similarly prefigures, through Harry's imagery of "the distant waterfall...half-heard" a few lines earlier, those passages in *Four Quartets* of greatest lyrical intensity and central motif, specifically the waterfall image in *The Dry Salvages* and *Little Gidding.*

But it is in *Burnt Norton,* the first Quartet, that the central motif of the rose-garden emerges most fully and is constituted as a standard of reference for our recognition of rose-garden elements elsewhere in Eliot's work, and in the sources that are claimed as well. This is, of course, the case for *The Secret Garden,* with its impressive cluster of elements: garden, bird, door, children. These are properties of the scene, or figures in the pattern. Another such figure is the word *quick,* as in "Quick, said the bird, find them, find them," and "Quick now, here now, always." There is a point in the novel where this word is conspicuous by its form in Yorkshire dialect, spoken by Dickon when he and Mary are first exploring the secret garden together:

> "That one?" she said. "Is that one quite alive—quite?"...
>
> "It's as wick as you or me," he said; and Mary remembered that Martha [the servant girl, Dickon's sister] had told her that "wick" meant "alive" or "lively."
>
> "I'm glad it's wick!" she cried out in her whisper. "I want them all to be wick. Let us go round the garden and count how many wick

ones there are."
    She quite panted with eagerness, and Dickon was as eager as she
was. They went from tree to tree and from bush to bush.[7]

The word, repeated and emphasized, while the quick and eager
children whisper cries, invites association between the scene in the
novel and the scene in *Burnt Norton*. But the novel has even more
cogent correspondences with that scene (as I call it). In the final
chapter (called "In the Garden" with at least double meaning) there is
an account of the long-sorrowing Archibald Craven as he wandered in
Europe, from Norway to Switzerland to Austria, and then a detailed
description of an experience in the Austrian Tyrol. After walking in a
wonderful valley there, he sat down to rest alongside a small stream.

> As he sat gazing into the clear running of the water, Archibald
> Craven gradually felt his mind and body both grow *quiet, as quiet as*
> the valley itself. He wondered if he were going to sleep, but he was
> not. He sat and gazed at the *sunlit water* and his eyes began to see
> things growing at its edge. There was one lovely mass of blue
> forget-me-nots growing so close to the stream that its leaves were wet
> and at these he found himself looking as he remembered he had
> looked at such things years ago. He was actually thinking tenderly
> how lovely it was and what wonders of blue its hundreds of little
> blossoms were. He did not know that just that simple thought was
> *slowly filling* his mind—*filling and filling* until other things were
> softly pushed aside. It was as if a sweet clear spring had begun to rise
> in a stagnant pool and had *risen and risen* until at last it swept the
> dark water away. But of course he did not think of this himself. He
> only knew that the valley seemed to grow *quieter and quieter* as he
> sat and stared at the bright delicate blueness. *He did not know how
> long* he sat there or what was happening to him, but at last he moved
> as if he were awakening and he got up slowly and stood on the moss
> carpet, drawing a long, deep, soft breath and wondering at himself.
> Something seemed to have been *unbound and released* in him, very
> *quietly*.[8]

The entire passage portrays clearly and vividly the experience of the
moment out of time which has often been noted in *Burnt Norton* and
other parts of Eliot's poetry, but I have added emphasis to words and
phrases which have a close and specific relevance to *Burnt Norton*, in
particular to these lines:

> And the pool was filled with water out of sunlight,
> And the lotos rose, quietly, quietly.

In Burnett's prose the *filling* and the *rising* are an analogy for what happens in the man's mind and this corresponds with the vision of water and lotos in Eliot's poem. Other details of correspondence are Burnett's "He did not know how long" and Eliot's (in Section II) "I cannot say, how long, for that is to place it in time." And again, Burnett's "unbound and released" and Eliot's "release from action and suffering." Such matching of details is meaningful because Burnett and Eliot describe experiences which have a common identity beyond the recurrence and likeness of a few words and phrases. When Burnett says—"I do not know enough ... to be able to explain how this had happened to him. Neither does anyone else yet"—she produces the paradox of having already described what is beyond explanation. This is like Eliot's paradox of the moment out of time that can be remembered "only in time."

During the period that followed the quasi-mystical experience when summer had turned into fall, Craven had a dream in which his young wife called him by name ("Archie") and repeated the phrase, "In the garden." Shortly after the dream, he read a letter summoning him to Misselthwaite, to which he proceeded promptly, and on arriving, soon made his way to the locked door of the garden:

> The ivy hung thick over the door, the key was buried under the shrubs, no human being had passed that portal for ten lonely years—and yet inside the garden there were sounds. They were the sounds of running scuffling feet seeming to chase round and round under the trees, they were strange sounds of lowered suppressed voices—exclamations and smothered joyous cries. It seemed actually like the laughter of young things, the uncontrollable laughter of children who were trying not to be heard but who in a moment or so—as their excitement mounted—would burst forth. What in heaven's name was he dreaming of—what in heaven's name did he hear? Was he losing his reason and thinking he heard things which were not for human ears? Was it that the far clear voice had meant?
>
> And then the moment came, the uncontrollable moment when the sounds forgot to hush themselves. The feet ran faster and faster— they were nearing the garden door—there was quick strong young breathing and a wild outbreak of laughing shouts which could not be contained—and the door in the wall was flung wide open, the sheet of ivy swinging back, and a boy burst through it at full speed and, without seeing the outsider, dashed almost into his arms.[9]

What are we to do with such coincidences? We can dismiss "the door in the wall" as truly and understandably a mere coincidence with H. G. Wells' story. Burnett was hardly echoing Wells. Yet her story contains certain passages which enter that region already well filled with possible sources. Eliot's imagery of "leaves...full of children,/Hidden excitedly, containing laughter" and "the hidden laughter/Of children in the foliage" may be felt as most clearly echoing this climactic scene of *The Secret Garden* with its "uncontrollable moment"—and with so much else in the novel at large that matches the cluster of images in *Burnt Norton* and reverberates in Eliot's work "before and after."

There is something more about *The Secret Garden* which matches something in Eliot's work other than the cluster of images. I am referring to a feature of the novel which is comparable to Eliot's plays after *Murder in the Cathedral*. Like the plays, the novel is primarily a story of contemporary secular experience, yet it contains a current of spirituality which becomes identified, late in the novel and then only briefly, with the Christian religion. The children's recurring references to the "Magic" by which both garden and children (Mary and Colin) are restored and revived are plausible and recognizable as characteristic of the childhood mentality. The chapter which tells of Mary and Dickon first bringing the invalid boy into the secret garden ends climactically with Colin's exclamation, "I shall get well! And I shall live forever and ever and ever!"—a statement which has religious implications beyond the speaker's intended meaning. Such implications are sharpened when we learn, in the final chapter of the novel, of a preternatural coincidence: that Colin's life-affirming exclamation occurred on the same day as the father's quasi-mystical experience as he rested by the Tyrolean stream. The implications had been expanded in the previous chapter when Colin repeated the affirmation and went on to say, "I feel as if I want to shout out something—something thankful, joyful!"—whereupon the old gardener suggested, "in his dryest grunt.... and he did not make the suggestion with any particular reverence," that Colin sing the Doxology. But Colin had never heard of the Doxology, so Dickon sang it:

> Praise God from whom all blessings flow,
> Praise him all creatures here below,
> Praise Him above ye Heavenly Host,
> Praise Father, Son, and Holy Ghost.
>   Amen.

Then Colin said, "It's a very nice song.... Perhaps it means just what I mean when I want to shout out that I'm thankful to the Magic." On Colin's request, Dickon repeated the song and they all joined in, Colin, Mary, and the old gardener.[10] Thus the idea and the experience of

Christian belief appear in the story with an almost incidental quality, unobtrusively, just that one time, and the story proceeds to its conclusion with other climaxes and in terms other than the specifically Christian. If the story yields Christian terms and meanings, it also holds to its own terms and meanings, as experienced by contemporary characters and described by the author. To say all this is to say that there is a respect in which *The Secret Garden* is an analogue for Eliot's plays, and therefore not inconceivably among such paradigms as lie behind the plays.

IX
Echo, Source, Influence

After dwelling so long on various kinds of sources for Eliot's poetry, it is time to consider whether these details are further evidence for what was already known—that Eliot's poetry is dense with echoes from other writers—or whether this evidence yields new meaning and new questions. I raise the subject in order to propose that some new issues do indeed arise. Some of these are a matter of emphasis: that Eliot's poetry is even more dense with echoes than anyone had thought; that Eliot echoes some writers (Milton, Benson, Conrad) more than had been realized. But there are implications and indications which go well beyond the matter of quantity, be it quantity of sources echoed or quantity of echoes from one source and another. There is also the question of what merit or demerit belongs to the investigations that I have made, as well as to such investigations in general.

This is a subject on which Eliot has commented more than once. Much of what I have been doing here, and what I and others have done in the past, follows the example of that classic of literary detection and discovery, the study of Coleridge's sources by John Livingston Lowes in *The Road to Xanadu*. Eliot referred to this work twice in his Norton lectures (1932–33), and again almost a quarter of a century later in the lecture "The Frontiers of Criticism" (1956). In one of the earlier lectures Eliot remarked: "Mr. Lowes has, I think, demonstrated the importance of instinctive and unconscious, as well as deliberate selection.... I should say that the mind of any poet would be mag-netized in its own way, to select automatically, in his reading ... the material—an image, a phrase, a word—which may be of use to him later."[1] This is surely a sound generalization, yet it applies in mark-edly greater degree to Coleridge and to Eliot (even though we must say: to each in his own way) than to other poets. In the final Norton lecture Eliot brought the Lowes demonstration closer to home. Speaking of "Kubla Khan," he said: "The imagery of that fragment, certainly, whatever its origins in Coleridge's reading, sank to the depth of Coleridge's feeling, was saturated, transformed there—'those are pearls that were his eyes'—and brought up into daylight again."[2]

The interjection of the line from Ariel's song in *The Tempest* is already saturated with a personal relevance for Eliot because the line is twice quoted in *The Waste Land* (ll. 48 and 125), so that we recognize that in speaking about Coleridge Eliot was being more than lightly implicit about himself. In fact, in the same paragraph Eliot went on to report that he had twice borrowed certain imagery from Chapman, who had in turn borrowed it from Seneca:

> There is first the probability that this imagery had some personal saturation value, so to speak, for Seneca; another for Chapman, and another for myself, who have borrowed it twice from Chapman. I suggest that what gives it such intensity as it has in each case is its saturation—I will not say with 'associations,' for I do not want to revert to Hartley—but with feelings too obscure for the authors even to know what they were.[3]

(These statements are themselves so saturated as to invite analysis at some length eventually, but I can't resist noting here the pseudo-naive assumption that "associations" are inevitably and merely associated with Hartley rather than, in 1933, more recent psychological theories.)

Eliot's later comments on Lowes's *The Road to Xanadu* reveal again his sensitivity to what he then called "the criticism of explanation by origins." In that lecture (1956) he coupled Lowes's book with Joyce's *Finnegans Wake* as "two books which have had, in this connection, a rather bad influence." By "this connection" he meant that "while Dr. Lowes has fired such practitioners of hermeneutics with emulative zeal, *Finnegans Wake* has provided them with a model of what they would like all literary works to be." Some parts of the argument are patently unconvincing. For example, there is the account of a person, "slightly touched in one corner of his head from having read *The Road to Xanadu*," who inquired whether "the dead cats of civilization," "rotten hippo" and Mr. Kurtz have a connection with "that corpse you planted last year in your garden"—"merely an earnest seeker," Eliot said, "trying to establish some connection between *The Waste Land* and Joseph Conrad's *Heart of Darkness*." But to deride such dead cats was no better than beating a dead horse, for indeed Mr. Kurtz and *Heart of Darkness* have a substantial connection with *The Waste Land*, as the world would have known from the start if Eliot had not heeded Pound's advice to remove the epigraph about Kurtz and the horror, which Eliot called at that time "the most appropriate I can find, and somewhat elucidative." In the same lecture there are other correctives that are just as patently misleading as the one about Conrad, such as calling the Notes to *The Waste Land* a "remarkable exposition of bogus scholarship," and saying "I regret having sent so many enquirers off on a wild goose chase after Tarot cards and the Holy Grail."[4] By "The Frontiers of Criticism" Eliot meant that criticism becomes less valuable and less justifiable when it becomes excessively explanatory and analytical of sources. The argument is reasonable in its own general terms, but Eliot's dwelling on Lowes's book as a bad influence reveals his own instinct to discourage traffic on the road to the waste land, the road to the rose-garden, the road to Little Gidding. It reveals—there is no avoiding the expression—Eliot's anxiety of influence. These were subjects, anxiety and influence, on which Eliot often commented, sometimes anticipating later elaborations. I make these observations in the hope that the terms have not been permanently captured by Harold Bloom's ambitious enterprise.

Eliot touched and dwelled on the subject of influences, sources, origins, throughout his entire career. This is a large concern in the early and famous essay "Tradition and the Individual Talent," where he made the oft-quoted statement that "not only the best, but the most individual parts of [a poet's] work may be those in which the dead poets, his ancestors, assert their immortality most vigorously."[5] In several of the *Selected Essays* Eliot spotted echoes and borrowings by the English dramatists from the plays of Seneca and from each other—and he made generalizations, as in "Philip Massinger" (1920): "Immature poets imitate; mature poets steal; bad poets deface what they take, and good poets make it into something better, or at least something different."[6] In a recent essay on Eliot's criticism, Roger Sharrock says, "This splendid epigrammatic sentence may be thought to embody almost all of what Harold Bloom had to say over fifty years later, with a great deal of posturing and neologism, in *The Anxiety of Influence*."[7] In the same essay Sharrock gives Eliot's criticism bad marks (along with good) on a number of counts, including posturing. But the essentially interesting thing is the comparing of Bloom and Eliot. Undoubtedly, Eliot had his anxieties, and sometimes they were anxieties of influence, but Bloom has conspicuously neglected to give these his authoritative attention. Could it be that he has been restrained by an anxiety that he has been influenced by insights and propositions scattered throughout a number of Eliot's early essays? Does Bloom dismiss Eliot's poetry as overrated and unworthy of attention because that poetry is too unwieldy for his systemic purposes—too unwieldy because the influences in Eliot's poetry come from too many directions and are so often at varying and indeterminable levels of awareness?

Just below the sentence Sharrock so much admires, Eliot said, "A good poet will usually borrow from authors remote in time, or alien in language, or diverse in interest." These remarks are obviously subjective, relevant to Eliot's own poetry, and they point to statements he made about influences on his own poetry. For example, in this statement on early influences, one is alien in language and another is remote in time: "The form in which I began to write, in 1908 or 1909, was directly drawn from the study of Laforgue together with the later Elizabethan drama; and I do not know anyone who started from exactly that point."[8] This sounds very precise and assured, perhaps too much so, but Eliot made a number of comments on the subject at different periods of his life, and it should not be surprising (or confusing) that there are differences in emphasis and even in substance. We don't expect that anyone can succeed in being wholly objective and consistent in so subjective a matter, or that the issue allows for a conclusion other than one which is qualified and inconclusive. Speaking in 1961 of his practice as a critic, Eliot said, "my own theorizing...springs from direct experience of those authors who have profoundly influenced my own writing.... I have written best about writers who have influenced my own poetry."[9] In the same lecture Eliot observed that he had written "nothing about Jules Laforgue, to whom I owe more than to any poet in any language.... The reason, I believe, is that no one commissioned me to do so." After thus acknowledging Laforgue, Eliot went on to say, "There is one poet...who impressed me profoundly when I was twenty-two,...one poet who remains the comfort and amazement of my age.... Dante."[10] In an earlier lecture, "What Dante Means to Me" (1950), he had also discussed the influence of these two poets in the same context, saying first of Dante, "I still, after forty years, regard his poetry as the most persistent and deepest influence upon my own verse.... " He then went on to say of Laforgue, "he was the first to teach me how to speak, to teach me the poetic possibiliities of my own idiom of speech."[11] There is not necessarily a contradiction between the greatest debt, acknowledged to Laforgue in 1961, and the deepest influence, granted to Dante in 1950, and even if there would appear to be a contradiction, it could be resolved by considering that Eliot was referring to different kinds of debts and influences, as well by the lapse in time between the two statements. The debt to Laforgue was acknowledged early on and more than once, yet by 1961 Eliot may have felt it deserved an emphasis he had never previously given. If Eliot wrote nothing about Laforgue during his early years as a critic, the reason may be not only that he was not so commissioned, but that the debt weighed too heavily.

The subject of influence in Eliot's own comment is worthy of more attention than I have given it, but I have made this limited survey to show that influence was a substantial and recurring subject in his criticism, and to show that at different times Eliot gave different emphases to the matter of influences on his own poetry. One meaning (among several) of what I call different emphases is that there are different kinds of influence and different degrees of influence. These terms are used loosely here, as they should be, for the nature of influence is not something that can be clearly categorized or precisely measured. Since Eliot gave emphatic acknowledgment to Laforgue and Dante, we may ask how these influences may be compared. Answers can be sought in more ways than I will attempt here, but I note the obvious fact that Laforgue and Dante, besides being different influences, were different kinds of influence. Dante's poetry was for Eliot an object of life-long admiration and of recurring reference in his prose and in his own poetry. Eliot aspired to partake of excellences which he found in Dante, and he consciously invited the reader to associate his poetry with Dante's, from the epigraph to "Prufrock" to the conspicuously Dantean terza-rima-like passage in Part II of *Little Gidding*—and to the statement in 1950 that Dante's poetry was "the most persistent and deepest influence." Laforgue was certainly not persistent in the way that Dante was, yet Eliot finally accorded him the greatest debt, so that he is a *deepest* influence too.

Dante's poetry was an influence which Eliot sought and cultivated throughout his career. Laforgue's poetry, like a few other "books," had an intense impact on Eliot at an early age and stage, an impact which produced an influence that has long been familiar. The point I wish to make is this—that some deep and enduring influences on Eliot and on his poetry came from an *early impact*. I deliberately give emphasis to both words, for I have come to believe that some of Eliot's early reading had impacts so sharp and strong that they produced indelible effects—influences—which show in his poetry early and late. Such effect and influence were produced by Arthur Symons' *The Symbolist Movement in Literature*, of which Eliot wrote in 1930: "I myself owe Mr. Symons a great debt. But for having read his book I should not, in the year 1908, have heard of Laforgue and Rimbaud; I should probably not have begun to read Verlaine, and but for reading Verlaine, I should not have heard of Corbière. So the Symons book is one of those which have affected the course of my life."[12] This statement gives Symons a great deal of credit, yet it can be misleading if it is taken to mean that Symons led Eliot to read one and another of the *symboliste* poets and to mean no more—for I share Elisabeth Schneider's conviction that "the *persona* influencing Eliot was at least as much Laforgue-through-Symons as it was Laforgue direct; most of the clearly Laforguian side of Eliot is in fact right there in Symons...."[13] This has been my own belief since the time I was writing the essay "Laforgue, Conrad and Eliot." Furthermore, I now believe that Eliot, who was always responsive to influences, was peculiarly and singularly responsive and impressionable during a short period of time early in his career—in 1908 and thereabouts. That is the period when he read Symons' chapter on Laforgue, when in all likelihood he read (along with other works of Conrad) *Heart of Darkness* and "The Return," and Benson's *FitzGerald*.

Benson's book is an especially good example of what I call early impact. This is so for a number of reasons. Because it is a book of very modest distinction and even less reputation, the *time* Eliot read it gains in importance as a feature of influence. It is unlikely that this is a book which Eliot read and re-read. The specifics of influence are miscellaneous: the portraits of Prufrock and of Gerontion owe common features to Benson's portrait of FitzGerald; the "Segismund" passage lies behind "A Game of Chess" as a source of details and as an example of complex echoing; Benson's comment on Omar and the wine-jar reverberates in the motif-passages of greatest intensity in *Four Quartets*. I recall these miscellaneous particulars of influence in order to argue that the impact of Benson's book owes something to the time Eliot read it. Implicit in my "theory" of impact is the idea that certain writing produced an immediate and lasting influence on Eliot, precipitating the personal material into terms derived from the sources of impact. Where Eliot spoke of the "form" of his early poetry "directly drawn from the study of Laforgue together with the later Elizabethan drama," I would propose that this form (meaning all aspects of style and effect) was initiated not so much by the study as by the impact of Laforgue—and others, especially FitzGerald, Benson, and Conrad. A common feature of these early influences is their continuing presence in later stages of Eliot's career. The Laforgue of Symons' chapter is echoed in *Murder in the Cathedral*.[14] FitzGerald, Benson, and Conrad are all echoed in poems of the *Prufrock* group, but they become (so to speak) steadily rising influences in the later stages of Eliot's career. This is especially true of FitzGerald's *Omar*, the earliest impact (in my opinion a basic and pervasive influence) the effects of which become increasingly apparent (as well as sea-changed) in Eliot's later poetry.

Was Eliot always conscious of echoing other writers at the time he wrote passages or words which are recognizably echoes? The question is easily answered: no, for all writers echo (borrow, derive, and so on) to greater or lesser degree and not always consciously. But Eliot echoed more than most, and in a way that made echoing a hallmark of his poetry and of his reputation as a poet. Obviously much of the echoing in his poetry was deliberate. It is impossible to say of any one echo that Eliot was not aware of it. My purpose here is to propose that Eliot was more than ordinarily given to echoing, that the echoing occurred naturally and involuntarily, even compulsively, in many cases consciously and in some cases not. He may have become aware of some echoes after the fact, and of others never. My meaning is that Eliot did not derive the technique of echoing, or of montage and collage, from Pound or Joyce or anyone else in any medium, although he may have been affected by their example. If Eliot developed a technique of echoing in his poetry and a justification for echoing in his criticism ("Tradition and the Individual Talent," etc.), the development followed from his natural impulse and his native habit. It followed too from his interest in literary influence as he found it in later Elizabethan drama, in *Paradise Lost,* and in various other writings.

A much quoted and much considered comment by Eliot on his own sources of influence is the passage in *Little Gidding* (II) where the poet speaks of meeting "some dead master/ . . . /Both one and many . . . / . . . a familiar compound ghost/Both intimate and unidentifiable." Despite the deliberately vague and ambiguous terms, critics have offered identifications of the "one" and the "compound" as writers ranging from Brunetto Latini and Dante to Yeats and Pound. To this large company I would add, without displacing or overlooking Conrad, Lawrence, Joyce and others—I would add FitzGerald and Benson. The exclamation, emphasis, and question of "What! are you here?" and the comment that these "words sufficed/To compel the recognition they preceded" imply a recognition which is also a surprise, so I propose that FitzGerald and Benson and the FitzGerald-Benson compound qualify as an adequate surprise. With this indeterminable speculation I associate the reference in *Little Gidding* (III) to "one who died blind and quiet." This has commonly and plausibly been understood as a reference to Milton, yet I recall the observation (but not the observer) that it could also mean Joyce. If that is so, it could even more readily mean FitzGerald. Eliot certainly remembered him as described by Benson, "in a dry month, old and blind, being read to by a country boy, longing for rain." He might also, at whatever level of awareness, have remembered Benson's brief account of FitzGerald's death: "it was found that he had died quietly in the night, as he had desired to die,"[15] and was thus certainly "one who died blind and quiet."

But if it is questionable whether the one who died blind and quiet is indeed one and many, there is much in Eliot's poetry that is properly so described. There are at least two kinds of multiple sources. In exploring the relationship between the "Segismund" passage and "A Game of Chess," I found instances where the source of Eliot's echo is itself the echo of an earlier source, even of a reverberating chain of echoes. Another kind occurs where diverse sources converge at a single echo-locus in Eliot's poetry. Such is the phrase "under a juniper tree" in Section II of *Ash Wednesday*, as shown in my essay on that poem. The sources are Grimm's tale "The Juniper Tree" and the account of the prophet Elijah who, after wandering in the wilderness, "sat down under a juniper tree" (I Kings 19:4). The question might be raised whether Grimm's tale echoes that point in the Bible. I think not, but there are cases where such question arises and cannot be resolved.

When Eliot says "Other echoes/Inhabit the garden," we cannot know for sure where all the echoes in the rose-garden begin and end. A simpler example is the well known line in *The Waste Land*, "I will show you fear in a handful of dust." It will be recalled that the final phrase occurs in Conrad's story "The Return": "He was afraid with that penetrating faltering fear that seems, in the very middle of a beat, to turn one's heart into a handful of dust." The phrase occurs again in Conrad's longer narrative *Youth*: "... I remember my youth and the feeling that will never come back any more ... the triumphant conviction of strength, the heat of life in the handful of dust...."[16] But the phrase occurs also in other and earlier writers. It is in Tennyson's *Maud* (Part II: V, i): "And my heart is a handful of dust...." And it is in Donne's *Devotions upon Emergent Occasions* (Meditation IV): "What's become of man's great extent and proportion when himself shrinks himself and consumes himself to a handful of dust." Some of the questions that arise are obvious. Was Tennyson echoing Donne (consciously or unconsciously)? Was Conrad echoing one, or both, and himself as well? Eliot had read *Maud* and "The Return," almost certainly *Youth* and Donne's Meditation. What is significant here is not so much whether Eliot was or was not aware of borrowing (or stealing) the phrase from one or another or all of the earlier writers, but the fact that here again the source is one and many, the echo has that extensive resonance which so often and so characteristically marks Eliot's poetry. It is also significant that it is Eliot's use of the phrase which, in the twentieth century, is a familiar quotation. Evelyn Waugh quoted the line as an epigraph to his novel *A Handful of Dust*. Some comment in the After-Notes to my essay "Laforgue, Conrad and

Eliot" bears on this subject: "I had vaguely surmised that the phrase came from the Bible.... I consulted Bible concordances and other appropriate dictionaries, but with negative results. The thirteenth edition of *Bartlett's Familiar Quotations* (1955) contains the phrase in its index, but the only reference is to the lines from *The Waste Land*, quoted in its section on Eliot."[17]

Our knowledge of the sources of echoes and influences in Eliot's poetry has implications which are many and diverse. One of these relates to the impression shared by Eliot and his readers at an early stage that the individuality and modernity of his poetry was nourished by sources remote in time (Dante, the metaphysical poets, the Elizabethan dramatists) and different in language (Laforgue and other French *symbolistes*). It is understandable that Eliot at that early stage preferred this image of the poet and the poetry. But it is clear, in my view, that Eliot's poetry at all stages partakes a large share of substance and style from his reading among writers in English of the nineteenth century and the early twentieth century: FitzGerald, Benson, Symons, Conrad, Lawrence—and, of course, writers that have not been mentioned in this essay. We know that he had read the writers just mentioned, but even if he had not read others, H. G. Wells and Frances Hodgson Burnett for example, the fact is that the correspondences exist, that there are essences of meaning and expression common to Wells' short story, Burnett's juvenile novel, and Eliot's *Four Quartets*. This is to say a number of things. Although in *Four Quartets* there are allusions to and borrowings from Dante, Dame Juliana of Norwich, the anonymous author of *The Cloud of Unknowing*, and St. John of the Cross, the poet arrives at the most deeply personal and most intensely lyrical effects and meanings in passages which correspond most immediately with certain modern writings, some of which he may never have read, such as those of Wells and Burnett. If he never read them, then the fact is an indication that Eliot's most essential sensibility and most deeply personal obsession were characteristic of his time, however much they were also the highly individual features of his own identity. If it is possible that he never read them, it is also possible (until proven otherwise) that he never read Wilde's "The Selfish Giant"—or other works claimed as sources which are not positively self-evident or conclusively documented. Part of Eliot's achievement was his success in producing a striking singularity when at the same time he was part of a broad current which was already moving before (and after) he came on the scene. In the famous essay about tradition, he said of that subject, "It cannot be inherited, and if you want it you must obtain it by great labor."[18] Some critics (especially British) have disputed the validity of this dictum, in some cases perceiving it as a kind of American agony. My point here is that Eliot's dictum is refuted (especially when removed from its context) by Eliot's own practice as a poet, which reveals Eliot as heir to traditions which he obtained effortlessly and even involuntarily. Needless to say, the essay, illuminating and essential as it remains in the body of Eliot's writing, was not a credo to which he adhered in his criticism or his poetry—although unquestionably Eliot confronted and engaged in great labor, as a poet, as a critic, and as a person.

X
Conclusion:
Echo, Mirror, Ghost

Think at last
We have not reached conclusion,...
"Gerontion"

I am drawn to this passage now because I am aware that we have not reached conclusion, and because one of my conclusions is that conclusions are delusions, or illusions, or at least only tentative and temporary. While Eliot's poetry has been long established, conclusions about it have been misguided, misinformed, uninformed, inconclusive and incomplete. Certainly this present discourse cannot be wholly free of any of these defects. That is one of my "conclusions." Only too much is enough, and one is not adequately alerted to a purpose without also being over-alerted. But hindsight proves that over-alertness and under-alertness may and do co-exist. (Alerted to alertness, I have in the course of this essay often been concerned whether I stray, in one direction or another, from the true path.) Alertness is a readiness for recognition. Another "conclusion" then is that the individual reader and the community of readers arrive at one and another stage of readiness only over periods of time. I am much impressed with this phenomenon. How could Robert L. Morris have read Conrad's "The Return" without seeing more of Eliot's sources than he found in the last few pages of the story? No less puzzling (or more puzzling) is the fact that I read Morris's article and then Conrad's story in 1953 seeing very little more than Morris had.

Such facts are less puzzling when I consider that it requires a combination of chance and time to bring to readers certain stages of readiness for recognition. I have said *chance* because I have in mind the experience which is called the shock of recognition. Such shocks may produce effects which are relieved and removed only with the passage of time. The shock may be so shocking as to make the recognition appear insecure, uncertain, unworthy of further or of serious attention. On the other hand, a mistaken identity may become a false-alarm leading to compounded error and much ado about nothing. I can imagine my own reading of Burnett's *Secret Garden* pursued far more insistently—in 1950, say, while Eliot smiled and smiled and was a villain.

But I wish to drop for awhile the subject of false alarm and pursue again the subject of justifiable shock, or unmistaken identity. My hobby-horse for such excursion is obviously Benson's *FitzGerald*. So I refer again to Zabel's letter, quoted in Matthiessen's footnote in 1941, where Zabel proposes that Benson's "whole book" influenced "not only 'Gerontion' but... other passages in his work of that time"— which must mean Eliot's poetry from *Prufrock* to *The Waste Land* inclusive. Zabel had definitely experienced a recognition, yet his statement of it in a private letter to a friend rather than in published form suggests a measure of reservation, a reluctance to appear extravagant. Matthiessen too showed discretion and moderation by quoting Zabel merely in a footnote in 1941, and in the 1947 edition of his widely known book on Eliot, again in a footnote, cautiously deleting "other passages in his work of that time."

When Zabel spoke of the "whole book" he was referring to Benson's "picture of FitzGerald in his pathetic, charming and impotent old age." This is not relevant to the "Segismund" passage. But that too is part of the whole book. Zabel might have skipped over it. All of us do that at times. The passage is quoted in a context where Benson speaks discouragingly of FitzGerald's work as a translator of Calderón. Or Zabel might have read it normally enough without being alerted to a recognition of the correspondences with "A Game of Chess," as he *was* alerted by the unmistakable source for "Gerontion." On the other hand, John Abbott Clark was alerted by his seeming discovery of that source and published an article of a dozen pages, preceding some of my own recognitions and supplying others—yet he missed the "Segismund" passage, possibly because he chose to skip reading it, or fell to nodding. Had he recognized "Segismund," his essay might have received more general recognition long ago. Certainly, most critics and exegetes of Eliot's poetry have skipped Clark's essay through being unaware of it (as I was, until aroused for the scent of Benson-Eliot and finding it in the Martin check-list)[1], or were unpersuaded and unimpressed. So the general assumption that the first two lines of "Gerontion" have no relevance to their source in Benson has been unwarranted and misleading. For example, Helen Gardner has spoken of them as among "striking examples" of "prose that set up the rhythm for a poem"[2]—this statement itself a striking example of reading into words something that isn't there (and overlooking something that is). Benson's original sentence partakes of the quality of FitzGerald's personal letters, mildly mellifluent and gently mocking, whereas the prevailing rhythm of "Gerontion" derives from the blank verse of later Elizabethan drama a brisk emphasis and nervous energy—until at the end of the poem there is a return to the Benson-FitzGerald mood and manner: "Thoughts of a dry brain in a dry season." It may appear implausibly far-fetched and uncritically wilful to suggest that the "Segismund" passage has a place somewhere behind the prevailing rhythm of "Gerontion," but is that suggestion any more wrongheaded (perhaps eventually plausible) than the notion that Benson's sentence is a "striking example" of "prose that set up the rhythm for a poem"?

I am aware of only a few readers of Benson's *FitzGerald* in recent decades. So I welcome this occasion to refer to Austin Warren's temperately elegant essay "The Happy, Vanished World of A. C. Benson,"[3] which portrays Benson as person and writer with critically measured sympathy. Warren mentions the *FitzGerald* only in passing, rating it below the *Pater*. Eliot is never mentioned—Warren is not concerned with the "Gerontion" source. But I dare presume that Austin Warren, so avowedly aware of T. S. Eliot and his work,[4] had read and possibly re-read *FitzGerald* without being struck by "Segismund."

As in the case of Clark's essay on Benson, I discovered Beringause's argument that Omar is a major source of *The Waste Land* only after I had been aroused to pursue such game. It is my impression that Beringause's essay has received even less notice (if any) than Clark's. This fact may be related to what I have called the effects of the shock of recognition and to the fear of being guilty of false alarm. Beringause offers some substantial evidence for a claim that *Omar* had an influence on *The Waste Land*, but he exaggerates in such a way as to protect himself from a forthright commitment, producing some uncertainty in the reader as to where Beringause's seriousness begins and ends: "*The Waste Land* is of much greater artistic and historic importance than any of its critics have guessed.... Study reveals its connection with Eliot's early reading: from Edward Fitzerald's [sic] *Rubáiyát of Omar Khayyám* and from James Thomson's *The City of Dreadful Night* Eliot abstracted themes, symbols, characters, setting, and form. Like Fitzgerald and Thomson, Eliot was not above expressing in print his concepts of love. Unlike the Victorians, however, Eliot hid his feelings. As a result, it is only with Fitzgerald and Thomson as guides that one can safely tread the maze of *The Waste Land*."[5] Such writing may be intended to tease the readers and the critics, but it also reveals a writer who hid *his* feelings by taking a posture which is not wholly and strictly serious. I have not claimed so much for *Omar*'s influence on *The Waste Land*, but I have claimed that it is a continuing influence throughout Eliot's poetry, and if I am not equally serious and confident about every detail offered, I have indeed become confident that the general proposition should be taken seriously.

As stated earlier, the density of determinable sources for Eliot's poetry is beyond the ordinary. My additions to the body of sources previously known may support the view that as a poet Eliot lacked the creative energy and independent resourcefulness of poets whose work unquestionably is not subject to the charge of being derivative. This view is true enough. We must grant that Eliot was derivative. Yet it may be claimed that Eliot was derivative in such a way as to make derivativeness his own singular and historical achievement. No amount of source-hunting and source-finding can undo the impact which Eliot's poetry has had on generations of readers and on the course of literature. What he repeated from a great variety of sources was repeated in a voice that was and is recognized as the voice which conveys the quality and meaning of human experience—as experienced and recorded by an individual personality with a distinct sensibility. This too is a shock of recognition—recognition of a meaningful voice, whether or not a source is also being recognized.

All this has been said before in a number of ways, but now it leads me to a different kind of consideration: that in Eliot's case we become aware that the sources do not make claims upon the poetry to reduce its status and effect, but that the poetry reclaims its sources. In doing so, it enlarges and enriches our experience. To my taste and by my standards, Conrad's "The Return" stands well by itself. So does Eliot's poetry. The fact of a relation between the poetry and the story is mutually enlivening. The relation is not coldly mechanical or even ingeniously contrived. It is innocently and genuinely dynamic, truly and enduringly experiential. This is not a generalization that is offered as covering all cases. It is a simplification, but not an over-simplification. There are passages of Eliot's poetry which have this relation with Conrad's story and which also use other sources in ways that are coldly mechanical and ingeniously contrived. Certainly this is true of "A Game of Chess," with its posted signals (enforced by Eliot's Notes) pointing toward Shakespeare, Milton, Virgil, Exodus. But there are also the relations with Conrad's "The Return," with the "Segismund" passage, and hence with FitzGerald and with Benson more generally. These relations are evidence of the fact that the mechanical and the contrived are controlled and charged by a momentum of feeling and meaning which exists below the level of consciousness and which is active before and after the occasion of "A Game of Chess"—a momentum which is active for the poet during his productive career and active for readers as we become informed and aware. If FitzGerald's "Segismund" and Benson's whole book do not stand by themselves as Conrad's story does, that impresses us so much the more with the associations, concerns, and sensibility which Eliot brought to the reading of such material and with which it was remembered, recalled, and echoed. It also tells us of the subjective dimension which is a reality of literature and of reading, no matter who is reading what. Furthermore, Benson's whole book, because it includes "Segismund" as well as sources for various parts of Eliot's work, is testimony (no less than Dante, maybe more!) for that continuity whereby the "whole" of a poet's "work is one poem"—of the "great poet," that is, because we feel that all the parts of his work are "united by one significant, consistent, and developing personality,"[6] to apply some of the words with which Eliot proclaimed the greatness of Shakespeare, for his comment on other poets was habitually reflexive, as he himself reported and as has long been apparent. There is no contradiction or even paradox in the fact that a diversity of sources—Dante, Shakespeare, Milton, FitzGerald, Benson, Laforgue, Conrad, Lawrence and others—recurs throughout Eliot's work in a diversity of ways. On the contrary, the recurring and expanding diversity is a test and a demonstration of the unity which was achieved "by one significant, consistent, and developing personality." The catalogue of sources can be viewed as evidence of Eliot's limitations and compulsions, but if these were disabilities of the personality, they were also distinctive features of the same personality by which the several parts of the work are united into the one poem. They are a side of the coin and they count in the deserved and acknowledged value. The course of this essay is itself one kind of illustration for the view of Eliot's work as one poem. It will be recalled that my initial and relatively simple objective was to propose that Four Quartets had a seminal origin in FitzGerald's Omar and that in pursuing that objective I have been led into an extensive and variegated realm of sources, several of them "new," for the entire range of Eliot's poetry, including the plays.

The subject of the one poem and its relation with a diversity of sources brings me back to the problem of discriminating between sources and influences—a problem about which I may have to remain inconclusive. If it is allowed that all influences are also sources, then how can we determine what sources are also influences? There are of course many sources and many echoes that must be clearly dismissed as nothing more than sources and echoes. Such are echoes out of a once-popular ragtime song, children's game-songs, other songs (Mrs. Porter and her daughter), Conan Doyle, a letter of Ruskin's, and all more or less simple, one-to-one echoes. On the other hand, there is Benson's whole book, referred to by Eliot once (and once only, in 1938) as "a Life of Edward Fitzgerald—I think the one in the 'English Men of Letters' series." This has the effect of dismissing Benson as the mere one-to-one source of the first two lines of "Gerontion"—whereas I have implied and stated that Benson's *FitzGerald* was one kind of major influence (before "Gerontion," before and after 1938). If I am correct, then it appears that Eliot was revealing (as noted earlier) some anxiety of influence. I believe he was, and I wonder at what level of consciousness he was ever aware of the (or an) influence of Benson's book. But I am more interested in the question of why he might have felt anxiety, and in offering an answer to the question. This is a subject that relates to other occasions. I have in mind the original epigraph to *The Waste Land,* the quotation from Conrad's *Heart of Darkness.* It is well known that this epigraph was removed and replaced with the passage from Petronius's *Satyricon* as the result of an exchange of letters between Eliot and Pound. Pound wrote, "I doubt if Conrad is weighty enough to stand the citation." Eliot replied: "Do you mean not use the Conrad quote or simply not put Conrad's name to it? It is much the most appropriate I can find, and somewhat elucidative."[7] Pound may have thought Eliot somewhat obtuse to miss the point at first regarding the meaning of "weighty enough." But Eliot yielded, and Petronius's Latin and Greek, although less appropriate and elucidative than Conrad's fairly recent English, was weighty enough. Later, of course, Eliot went on the record for Conrad and *Heart of Darkness* with the epigraph to *The Hollow Men,* by which Conrad is made the weightier for *not* being named. With the epigraphs from Conrad, Eliot was acknowledging an influence, and I see no reason to conclude that such acknowledgment was made purely from anxiety—more likely it was free of anxiety. Conrad was weighty enough to be recognized as an influence—by Eliot, and eventually by others. B. C. Southam's comments, quoted earlier, are again relevant: "Next to Dante, Conrad's story is arguably the most important single literary experience in Eliot's poetry from 'Prufrock' onwards.... Conrad's nightmare vision would have made sense to Dante; and one would judge that these two writers were felt by Eliot to exert a single force flowing into and impowering his imagination."[8] Southam approaches his claim with obvious caution: "Next to Dante" means "after Dante," and the claim for *Heart of Darkness* is offered only "arguably," and finally, "one would judge" that Dante and Conrad were for Eliot "a single force." For Southam, Conrad was weighty enough to be recognized and acknowledged as a major influence, as he was for me. What, then, about A. C. Benson? Zabel recognized a prevailing influence but acknowledged it only in a personal letter to Matthiessen, who was minimally impressed, and eventually even so dubious as to "protect" Zabel from appearing to claim too much. Obviously, I have been claiming a great deal for Benson's whole book as a major influence on Eliot, and others will have to judge whether it is too much. But whether this influence is in fact greater or lesser, I want to observe that a problem arises when there has been substantial influence from a source so unweighty as Benson. For Eliot, there may have been a problem of anxiety, of disinclination to avow or even to recognize so extensive an influence. Others, the rest of us, have so far been unprepared and unwilling to experience the recognition. My earlier speculation, that there was a period of time, 1908 and thereabouts, when Eliot was subject to forceful and enduring impact from some of his reading, implies that some books (Benson, Arthur Symons) have had great influence on Eliot by an accident of time (or timing), while the books remain outside an established and timeless canon—which includes Dante and Conrad and T. S. Eliot. (I wish to add that it is not my concern here to uphold or to "deconstruct" the concept of the canonical, although I am aware that I have been moving in a realm where this issue is encountered.)

When first considering Southam's proposition that Dante and Conrad "were felt by Eliot to exert a single force flowing into and impowering his imagination," I demurred at the exclusiveness of this idea and said in effect that any number of influences as a single force was a more appealing idea. I mean that insofar as there is a *single force*, it is the force of the personality which receives the influences—that the influences, like the separate works of a poet's career, are "united by one significant, consistent and developing personality." If Dante and Conrad are parts of a force that is flowing in "Prufrock," so are Laforgue and Symons, and so are FitzGerald and Benson. Think from how many sources "a single force" may be flowing into the rose-garden of Eliot's poetry: Dante, Milton, FitzGerald, Benson, Conrad, Lawrence (Kipling, Wilde, Wells, Burnett?).

"Single force" is of course a metaphor, not even my own, and I would not want to rest on it too heavily—especially since I am interested in offering another kind of emphasis. This is that influences should be considered not only as they compare or equate in degree, but also as they differ in kind—and I hope that I have succeeded in clarifying this order of difference in some measure. Dante, Conrad, Benson (or Benson's whole book)—each was an influence and a kind of influence. Eliot didn't study and echo Conrad and Benson the way he studied and echoed Dante. It may be said that every echo of Dante is also an occasion of homage to Dante. This is not a generalization that can be applied to Conrad, although there is some homage to Conrad. But there is definitely no homage to Benson. Thus homage is an aspect of difference in the kind of influence. So there are different kinds of influence, and I now dare say that Dante was not a greater influence on Eliot than Conrad, Dante was not a greater influence than Laforgue (Eliot said so), Dante was not a greater influence than Benson. Different, yes; greater, no.

Some of the terms which I have been using (either borrowed or conventional) are useful for comparing FitzGerald and Benson as influences on Eliot. It may, for example, be said that they are a single force, a confluence—especially as we keep in mind that FitzGerald's "Segismund" is contained in Benson's book, and then recall too "the voice of music, the song of the bird, the whisper of leaves, the murmur of the hidden stream"—as the passage resonates out of FitzGerald's *Omar* and into Eliot's *Four Quartets*. The issue is really between FitzGerald's famous poem and Benson's obscure and neglected book. Because Eliot had read one (which he praised uniquely for its effect on him as a boy), he also read the other (which he slighted in seeming to recall it uncertainly, not even naming the author). Yet Benson's book, far less weighty than FitzGerald's poem, may be regarded as the greater influence because it is documented more substantially and more precisely—by the "Gerontion" source, by "Segismund," by the passage of Omaresque prose. But I prefer to put an emphasis on difference in the kind of influence rather than on quantitative degree of influence, and I think that the FitzGerald-Benson case is especially illuminating for the value of this emphasis. "Segismund," a "new source," serves so well the view that I am taking. FitzGerald's Elizabethan-Miltonic adaptation of Calderón's Spanish, encountered by Eliot in Benson's book, sharing some ambient features with Conrad's prose, is a striking example and occasion of different kinds of influences which "exert a single force" because they flow, not just *into* but *within*, the one personality of the poet T. S. Eliot.

As a final illustration of this argument, I call attention again to "Segismund" as a new source in a respect not yet mentioned and as an influence flowing within the poet and the poetry. I have in mind the mirror imagery which FitzGerald derived from Book IV of *Paradise*

Lost and which led me to a re-reading of Conrad's "The Return" and to new recognitions of correspondences with Eliot's poetry. As noted earlier, there is a mirror in "A Game of Chess": the glass which doubled the flames of the candelabra. But this is not the mirror experience of Eve in Book IV or of Conrad's protagonist in "The Return"—or of Segismund as he reports it, after telling of the pictures on the wall:

> and one most strange of all
> That, as I pass'd the crystal on the wall,
> Look'd from it—left it—and as I return,
> Returns, and looks me face to face again—
> Unless some false reflection of my brain,
> The outward semblance of myself.—Myself?
> How know that tawdry shadow for myself,
> But that it moves as I move; lifts his hand
> With mine; each motion echoing so close
> The immediate suggestion of the will
> In which myself I recognise—Myself!

But Eliot does give versions of the experience in *Murder in The Cathedral* and in *Four Quartets*—once in *Burnt Norton*, and twice in *Little Gidding*. In Section I of *Burnt Norton*, there is the pool "filled with water out of sunlight":

> The surface glittered out of heart of light
> And they were behind us, reflected in the pool.

Among the echoes that inhabit the garden, there is here an echo of the pool-mirror experience of *Paradise Lost*, Book IV. There has not to my knowledge been a definitive explanation of *they* and *them* and *we* and *us* in this passage. Moreover, I regard the pronouns as *suggestive* and beyond any ultimate *definitive*. So my point here is that the pool and the reflections are themselves echoes and reflections of Milton's Garden of Eden, "our first world." This association for the garden of *Burnt Norton* (the rose-garden) has been made before, but not with reference to the reflecting pool.

The pool is itself a reflection in more than one sense: it is the mental experience of contemplation and meditation, and it is a reminiscent mirage "filled with water out of sunlight." It is related, moreover, to a comparable image in the opening lines of *Little Gidding*, where "The brief sun flames the ice" of frozen ditch-water, "Reflecting in a watery mirror/A glare that is blindness in the early afternoon." These two mirror images, each in its own phantasmic garden, bestow on each other a special measure of emphasis, for they are details which participate in a complex of correspondences. The opening passage of *Little Gidding* is dense with dynamic associations within *Four Quartets* and within the larger body of Eliot's verse. For example, the passage itself is an expanded echoing of words spoken by the First Tempter to Thomas in *Murder in the Cathedral*:

> Spring has come in winter. Snow in the branches
> Shall float as sweet as blossoms. Ice along the ditches
> Mirror the sunlight. Love in the orchard
> Send the sap shooting.

In *Little Gidding* it is "The soul's sap quivers," so that the expanded echoing is also a significant contrast. Another example is the Hyacinth garden of *The Waste Land*: "I could not/Speak, and my eyes failed, ... / ... /Looking into the heart of light, the silence," which corresponds with "glare that is blindness in the early afternoon." As has often been noted (along with reference to Conrad's *Heart of Darkness*), the phrase "heart of light" is repeated in the line of *Burnt Norton*, "The surface glittered out of heart of light." It is impressively relevant that in the opening passage of *Little Gidding* the statement, "Now the hedgerow/Is blanched for an hour with transitory blossom ... ," in an early draft was "Now the hedgerow/Glitters ... ," and so on.[9] At this stage one may readily (or too readily?) recall "The glitter of her jewels" ("A Game of Chess"), and perhaps even the "glittering caparison" of Segismund's servants. It is obvious not only that *Burnt Norton* is modeled on *The Waste Land* and the other Quartets on *Burnt Norton* in the larger outlines of form, but that the correspondences are at times specific and intricate—as they are in the case of interrelationship among the Hyacinth garden, the rose garden (and lotos pool) and midwinter spring—to signalize a formidable complexity by such brief and familiar references. The frozen ditch-water of *Murder in the Cathedral* and *Little Gidding* seems at a far remove from the narcissistic pool of Milton's Book IV, but from that pool a current does indeed flow, over a varied and extensive terrain, through the rose-garden of *Burnt Norton,* and into the ditches. Merging with this current is the Yeatsean current which critics have located (and Eliot has acknowledged) in *Little Gidding*—in this case specifically "the frog-spawn of a blind man's ditch" ("A Dialogue of Self and Soul," II). Yeatsean too may be the line "Not in the scheme of generation," echoing "Those dying generations" of "Sailing to Byzantium," echoing not just the word but essential meanings of the larger contexts, so that Eliot's

"Zero summer" compares with "the holy city of Byzantium" and the "artifice of eternity" in the respect that all of these are "not in time's covenant." These associations with Yeats are supported by the accepted presence of Yeats in the Dantean passage of Section II—or, in another perspective, the Dantean passage acknowledges the earlier presence of Yeats. In her book *The Composition of Four Quarters,* Helen Gardner states that "...the drafts make it clear that he began with Yeats in mind and worked toward a greater generality,"[10] and she demonstrates this point by collocating passages of the drafts with passages from Eliot's lecture on Yeats, and by quotations from and references to Yeats's poems: "The Spur," "An Acre of Grass," "Vacillation" V, and "Sailing to Byzantium." To these I would add "A Dialogue of Self and Soul." Once the relationship with Yeats is established, this poem becomes strikingly relevant. In fact, no other single poem of Yeats corresponds so extensively. Eliot's dialogue with "some dead master" is also a dialogue within the identity of the poet himself, such as declared by the descriptive title of Yeats's poem. Both poets look back on past experience, recognizing and judging their own misdeeds. Eliot's "rending pain of re-enactment/Of all that you have done and been ... " corresponds with Yeats's "What matter if I live it all once more?"—"I am content to follow to its source/Every event in action or in thought..." —and "I am content to live it all again/And yet again, if it be life to pitch/Into the frog-spawn of a blind man's ditch" (respectively from stanzas one, four and three of section II). Although "blind man's ditch" is a commonplace and even proverbial phrase (and as such a typical element of Yeats's later style), it corresponds with the frozen ditch water which reflects "A glare that is blindness in the early afternoon" of the opening of *Little Gidding.* In any event, it was this correspondence which called to my attention Yeats's "Dialogue of Self and Soul," so that I regard the phrase, however commonplace, as participating in a larger pattern of correspondences.

As for the reflections in *Burnt Norton* ("they were behind us"), these prefigure the "compound ghost" and the "double part" of *Little Gidding,* Section II:

> And as I fixed upon the down-turned face
> That pointed scrutiny with which we challenge
>   The first-met stranger in the waning dusk
>   I caught the sudden look of some dead master
> Whom I had known, forgotten, half recalled
>   Both one and many; in the brown baked features
>   The eyes of a familiar compound ghost

> Both intimate and unidentifiable.
> So I assumed a double part, and cried
> And heard another's voice cry: 'What! are you here?'

There is no literal and concrete mirror here, but among all the ghosts, there is also the ghost of a mirror—the mirror in which Segismund saw his "each motion echoing." This metaphorical merging of mirror and echo is appropriate to our recognition of Segismund's mirror echoed in Eliot's poem, when the poet "assumed a double part, and cried/And heard another's voice cry: 'What! are you here?'" Just as Segismund's motion is echoed, so the poet's cry is mirrored by a double part because the question—"What! are you here?" is a double question, in a sense not echoed, but simultaneously uttered and heard, an audio-vocal mirror experience where the voice is both one and many. It is the poet, younger and older, and among others, Benson, Calderón, FitzGerald, Omar Khayyám, a compound ghost who answers to many names, including Segismund.[11]

In closing this essay I feel obliged to proffer some generalization about what I have been doing—and not been doing. There are points at which I theorize about one matter and another regarding specifics and generalities of literary influence. It has not been my intention, however, to approach or to produce a theory of literature or a theory of literary influence—although I feel somewhat uneasily close to im- plying a theory of theories. If that is so, it is the theory that literature and the study of literature should not give rise to a system of ideas which is considered conclusive and exhaustive, which tends to absorb the literature from which it arose into the abstractions of a theory and its system, which responds to new literature, new infor- mation and new perspectives with Procrustean surgery, Ptolemaic accommodation or theological apologetics. Nonetheless, theorists will arrive and theories will arise. There will be battles of ideas and, what is worse, dirty politics. But the theories and the theorists (alas!) come and go, and as they do we are free to borrow vocabularies and to invent metaphors from their systems and from their remains— vocabularies and metaphors which may serve us, if we choose, in our study and experience of literature.

> On a huge hill,
> Cragged and steep, Truth stands, and he that will
> Reach her, about must, and about must go;
> And what the hill's suddenness resists, win so.

Myself when young did eagerly frequent
Doctor and Saint and heard great argument
    About it and about: but evermore
Came out by the same door wherein I went.

Hill-climbing is good exercise, even when we don't quite make it to the top. As for the same door, there is something very reassuring about that.[12]

Notes

Chapter I

1. "From Poe to Valery," *To Criticize the Critic* (New York: Farrar, Straus & Giroux, 1965), p. 27.

2. See Richard D. Altick, *The Art of Literary Research* (Revised Edition) (New York: W. W. Norton & Co., 1975), pp. 239–46, 280–82.

3. Introduction to Ezra Pound's *Selected Poems* (London: Faber and Gwyer, 1928), p. viii.

4. Altick, p. 112.

5. Hugh Kenner, *The Invisible Poet: T. S. Eliot* (New York: McDowell, Obolensky, 1959), pp. 136–37.

6. F. O. Matthiessen, *The Achievement of T. S. Eliot* (Second Edition) (New York & London: Oxford University Press, 1958), p. 42.

7. André Morize, *Problems and Methods of Literary History* (Boston: Ginn & Co., 1922), p. 229.

8. Harry Blamires, *Word Unheard: A Guide through Eliot's Four Quartets* (London: Methuen & Co., 1969), pp. 181–82. For more comment on this subject, see also his Appendix II and Index entries for *Hiawatha*.

9. *Huckleberry Finn* (London: The Cresset Press, 1950). For extended comment see Lois A. Cuddy, "Eliot and *Huck Finn*: River and Sea in *The Dry Salvages*," *T. S. Eliot Review*, vol. 3 (1976), pp. 3–11.

10. "American Literature and the American Language," *To Criticize the Critic*, p. 54.

11. Helen Gardner, *The Art of T. S. Eliot* (New York: E. P. Dutton & Co., 1950), pp. 159–60.

12. Elisabeth Schneider, *T. S. Eliot: The Pattern in the Carpet* (Berkeley and Los Angeles: University of California Press, 1975), pp. 160–62.

13. H. Gardner, *The Composition of Four Quartets* (New York: Oxford University Press, 1978), p. 39.

14. "Tradition and the Individual Talent," *Selected Essays* (New York: Harcourt, Brace and Co., 1932), p. 8.

15. "What Dante Means to Me," *To Criticize the Critic*, p. 126.

16. Ibid., p. 132.

17. The title essay in *To Criticize the Critic*, pp. 22, 23.

18. Philip R. Headings, *T. S. Eliot* (New York: Twayne, 1964), p. 32.

19. Grover Smith, *T. S. Eliot's Poetry and Plays: A Study in Sources and Meaning* (Chicago: University of Chicago Press, 1956), pp. 16, 17.

20. Kenner, *Invisible Poet*, p. 10.

21. *The Divine Comedy* (Carlyle-Wicksteed translation) (New York: Modern Library, 1932), p. 147.

22. Ibid., p. 148.

23. Matthiessen, *Achievement of Eliot*, p. 70.

24. See my T. S. Eliot: Moments and Patterns (Minneapolis: University of Minnesota Press, 1961), pp. 12–13.

25. Smith, Sources and Meaning, p. 26. See Smith's index entries under Henry James for comment on "Crapy Cornelia" and other stories and novels relevant to Eliot's poems.

26. Quoted (but unnamed) in Stanley Weintraub, The London Yankees (New York: Harcourt Brace Jovanovich, 1979), p. 358.

27. Smith, Sources and Meaning, p. 15.

28. Kristian Smidt, The Importance of Recognition (Trøms: Trykk: A. S. Peder Norbye, 1973), p. 81.

29. "The Three Voices of Poetry," On Poetry and Poets (New York: Farrar, Straus and Cudahy, 1957), p. 103.

30. The title essay in To Criticize the Critic, p. 20.

31. The Complete Poems and Plays 1909–1950 (New York: Harcourt, Brace and World, 1952), p. 54.

32. J. Hillis Miller, Poets of Reality (paper) (New York: Atheneum, 1969), pp. 137, 139.

33. Kenner, Invisible Poet, p. 44.

34. "John Ford," Selected Essays, p. 179.

35. See Donald Hall's interview with Eliot in The Paris Review, 21 (Spring-Summer 1959), p. 58.

36. See Gardner, Composition of Four Quartets, p. 180.

Chapter II

1. Blamires, Word Unheard, p. 2.

2. For an extended study, see R. A. Day, "Joyce's Waste Land and Eliot's Unknown God," Literary Monographs, vol. 4 (Madison, Wis.: 1971), pp. 139–226.

3. "Notes on Ash Wednesday," The Southern Review, IV, 4(1938–39), pp. 745–70. This is re-printed as "Ash Wednesday" in my book T. S. Eliot: Moments and Patterns.

4. W. T. Moynihan, "Character and Action in The Four Quartets," Mosiac, VI, 1 (Fall 1972), pp. 212, 227.

5. Hugh Kenner, "Eliot and the Tradition of the Anonymous," College English, 28 (May, 1967), pp. 560–61.

6. Hugh Kenner, The Pound Era (Berkeley: University of California Press, 1971), p. 438.

7. Donald Davie, "Anglican Eliot" in Eliot in His Time: Essays on the Fiftieth Anniversary of The Waste Land, ed. A. Walton Litz (Princeton, N.J.: Princeton University Press, 1973), pp. 191–94.

8. George T. Wright, "Eliot Written in a Country Churchyard: The Elegy and Four Quartets," English Literary History, 43 (1976), pp. 227–43.

9. The Use of Poetry and the Use of Criticism (London: Faber and Faber, 1933), p. 33. Hereafter I will omit sic in such cases ("Fitzgerald").

10. Ibid., p. 91.

11. A. C. Benson, Edward FitzGerald (London: MacMillan, 1905), p. 142.

12. Ibid., p. 29. Smith, Sources and Meanings, p. 63.

13. Kenner, Invisible Poet, p. 124.

14. Kenner, "Tradition of the Anonymous," p. 561.

15. F. O. Matthiessen, American Renaissance (New York: Oxford, 1941), p. 366.

16. In Matthiessen, Achievement of Eliot, pp. 73–74.

17. "On a Recent Piece of Criticism," Purpose, X, 2(1938), p. 93.

18. In The South Atlantic Quarterly, XLVIII (April 1949).

19. Clark, "Benson's FitzGerald," p. 261.

20. Ibid., p. 267.

21. Beringause, "Journey through *The Waste Land,*" *The South Atlantic Quarterly,* LVI (Jan. 1957), p. 79.

22. Benson, *FitzGerald,* pp. 1, 170.

23. Ibid., p. 163.

24. Ibid., p. 165.

25. Ibid., p. 80.

26. Ibid., pp. 189–90.

27. Ibid., pp. 190–91.

28. Ibid., p. 159.

29. Ibid., p. 115.

Chapter III

1. *Rubáiyát of Omar Khayyám,* ed. L. Untermeyer (New York: Random House, 1947), p. 124. When first engaged with the subject of Eliot and FitzGerald's translation, I "re-read" the poem in *The Norton Anthology* (see f.n. 2 below), which takes its text (the fifth version) from *The Variorum and Definitive Edition of Poetical and Prose Writings of Edward FitzGerald,* ed. George Bentham, 7 vols. (New York: Doubleday, 1902–3). Because this was inaccessible, I have used Untermeyer's edition (which is well equipped and generally available) for all page references to the poem and to FitzGerald's Preface and Notes. I use Arabic numerals to indicate stanzas of the fifth version of *Omar,* of which there are numerous editions.

2. As quoted in *The Norton Anthology of English Literature,* Revised, Vol. 2, ed. M. H. Abrams, et al. (New York: Norton, 1968), p. 1179.

3. Kenner, *Invisible Poet,* pp. 124–25.

4. Wright, "*Elegy* and *Four Quartets,*" p. 233. FitzGerald's phrase is from stanza 66 of *Omar.*

5. Arthur Symons, *The Symbolist Movement in Literature* (paperback) (New York: Dutton, 1958), p. 60.

6. *Omar,* p. 138.

7. Many editions and anthologies provide this information.

8. A convenient source of such information is J. R. Tutin, *A Concordance to FitzGerald's Translation of The Rubáiyát of Omar Khayyám* (London: Macmillan, 1900).

9. *Omar,* p. 139.

10. Ibid., pp. 129, 132.

11. Benson, *FitzGerald,* pp. 112, 113.

12. Robert Graves and Omar Ali-Shah, *The Rubáiyát of Omar Khayám: A New Translation with Critical Commentaries* (London: Cassell, 1967), p. 2.

13. L. P. Ewell-Sutton, "Sufism and Pseudo-Sufism," *Encounter,* XLIV, 5 (May 1975), p. 11.

14. David Ward, *T. S. Eliot Between Two Worlds* (London: Routledge and Kegan Paul, 1973), p. 231.

15. Benson, *FitzGerald,* p. 97.

Chapter IV

1. In Benson, *FitzGerald,* pp. 129–30.

2. Ibid., p. 130.

3. W. F. Prideaux, *Notes for a Bibliography of Edward FitzGerald* (London, 1901; rpt.

New York: Burt Franklin, 1968), p. 25.

4. John Milton, *Paradise Lost,* ed. Scott Elledge (New York: Norton, 1957).

5. Giorgio Melchiori, *The Tightrope Walkers* (New York: Macmillan, 1956), p. 55.

6. *The Poems of John Keats,* ed. Jack Stillinger (Cambridge: The Belknap Press of Harvard University Press, 1978), pp. 471–72.

7. Laura Riding and Robert Graves, *A Survey of Modernist Poetry* (Garden City: Doubleday, Doran, 1928), p. 170.

8. Melchiori, *Tightrope Walkers,* pp. 56–57.

9. A. Bartlett Giamatti, *The Earthly Paradise and the Renaissance Epic* (Princeton: Princeton University Press, 1966), p. 300.

10. Ward, *Eliot Between Two Worlds,* p. 95.

Chapter V

1. Robert L. Morris, "Eliot's 'Game of Chess' and Conrad's 'The Return'," *Modern Language Notes,* LXV, 6 (June, 1950), pp. 422–23.

2. Joseph Conrad, *Tales of Unrest* (Garden City, N.Y.: Doubleday, Page, 1920), pp. 308, 312–13. All my references for "The Return" are to this volume.

3. Ibid., pp. 230–31.

4. Ibid., pp. 212–13.

5. Ibid., p. 228.

6. Ibid., pp. 210–11.

7. Ibid., pp. 291–92.

8. Ibid., p. 233.

9. Ibid., pp. 215–16. I found comparable sources for "Preludes" in *Heart of Darkness,* as indicated in my book *T. S. Eliot: Moments and Patterns,* pp. 113–14.

10. Conrad, *Tales,* pp. 282–83.

11. Ibid., pp. 220–21.

12. Ibid., p. 269.

13. *Complete Poems and Plays,* p. 249.

14. Conrad, *Tales,* p. 228.

15. Ibid., p. 271.

16. B. C. Southam, *A Guide to the Selected Poems of T. S. Eliot* (New York: Harcourt, Brace and World, 1969, paperback), pp. 100, 23.

Chapter VI

1. A. C. Benson, *Walter Pater* (New York: Macmillan, 1960), p. 220.

2. *Use of Poetry and Criticism,* p. 146.

3. Ibid., p. 147.

4. Lowes, *The Road to Xanadu* (Boston: Houghton Mifflin, 1927), p. 343. See also Lane Cooper, "The Abyssinian Paradise in Coleridge and Milton," *Modern Philology* III (1905–6), pp. 327–32; and Joseph E. Duncan, *Milton's Earthly Paradise* (Minneapolis: University of Minnesota Press, 1972), pp. 196–97.

5. C. K. Stead, *The New Poetic* (London: Hutchinson, 1964), pp. 149, 151.

6. For an account of Miltonic elements in *Four Quartets,* see B. Rajan, "Milton and Eliot: A Twentieth-Century Acknowledgment," in *Milton Studies IX: The Presence of Milton,* ed. B. Rajan (Pittsburgh: University of Pittsburgh Press, 1978), pp. 115–29.

7. Benson, *Pater,* p. 18.

8. Melchiori, *Tightrope Walkers,* p. 93.

9. D. H. Lawrence, *Selected Literary Criticism* (London: Heinemann, 1955), pp. 84–89.

10. Ibid., pp. 88–89.

11. Ibid., pp. 85–86.

Chapter VII

1. The essays "Ash Wednesday" and "The Rose-Garden" are in my book *T. S. Eliot: Moments and Patterns*.

2. "The Wheel and the Point: Aspects of Imagery and Theme in Eliot's Later Poetry," *The Sewanee Review*, Winter 1947, pp. 126–47. This essay is reprinted in the book (which I edited) *T. S. Eliot: A Selected Critique* (New York: Rinehart, 1948); see pp. 448–49.

3. Quoted from the Norton Critical Edition (1971, ed. D. H. Gray), pp. 9–10.

4. Ibid., p. 61.

5. Lawrence, *The Complete Short Stories* (London: Heinemann, 1955), vol. I, pp. 225–26.

6. Martz, in my *Selected Critique*, p. 48.

7. Gardner, *Art of Eliot*, pp. 159–60. This statement was originally (and only) a footnote in Gardner's essay "Four Quartets: A Commentary," in B. Rajan (ed.), *T. S. Eliot, A Study of His Writings by Several Hands, Focus Three* (London, Dennis Dobson, 1947), p. 62.

8. *A Choice of Kipling's Prose*, ed. W. Somerset Maugham (London: Macmillan, 1952), pp. 233–34.

9. Schneider, *Pattern in the Carpet*, pp. 161–62.

10. Oscar Wilde, *The Happy Prince and Other Tales* (Boston: Roberts Brothers, 1888), pp. 49–50.

11. Gardner, *Composition of Four Quartets*, p. 40.

12. Grover Smith (p. 325) calls Wells' story a "good analogue of the rose-garden theme. "The Door in the Wall" was first published in *The London Daily Chronicle*, July 14, 1906; first reprinted in *The Country of the Blind and Other Stories*, T. Nelson and Sons, London 1911. My references are to *The Short Stories of H. G. Wells* (London: Ernest Benn, 1927).

13. Wells, p. 165.

14. Ibid., pp. 167–71.

15. Ibid., pp. 182–83.

16. *Selected Essays*, pp. 233–34.

17. As reported by Schneider, *Pattern in the Carpet*, p. 161.

18. Ibid., pp. 161–62.

19. As reported by Walter J. Ong, "Burnt Norton in St. Louis," *American Literature*, vol. 33 (1962), pp. 522–26.

20. Dennis Donoghue, *Thieves of Fire* (London: Faber and Faber, 1973), pp. 134–35.

21. I quote from the Doubleday, Page edition (1923), where it is stated that the novel was copyrighted in 1916 by Metropolitan Magazine Co.

Chapter VIII

1. *The Confidential Clerk* (New York: Harcourt, Brace, 1954), p. 12.

2. Frances Hodgson Burnett, *The Secret Garden* (New York: Lippincott, 1962), pp. 83–84.

3. Ibid., pp. 63–64.

4. Ibid., p. 80.

5. Ibid., pp. 59–60, 210.

6. In Eliot's *Complete Poems and Plays*, p. 251.

7. Burnett, *Secret Garden*, p. 93.
8. Ibid., p. 245.
9. Ibid., p. 252.
10. Ibid., pp. 234–36.

Chapter IX

1. *Use of Poetry and Criticism*, p. 78.
2. Ibid., p. 146.
3. Ibid., pp. 147–48.
4. *On Poetry and Poets* (New York: Farrar, Straus and Cudahy, 1957) pp. 118–22.
5. *Selected Essays*, p. 4.
6. Ibid., p. 182.
7. Roger Sharrock, "Eliot's 'Tone'," in D. Newton-DeMolina, *The Literary Criticism of T. S. Eliot* (London: The Athlone Press, 1977), p. 171.
8. In the Introduction to Ezra Pound's *Selected Poems* (London: Faber and Gwyer, 1928), p. viii.
9. *To Criticize the Critic*, p. 20.
10. Ibid., p. 21.
11. Ibid., pp. 125–26.
12. *The Criterion*, IX (Jan. 1930).
13. Schneider, *Pattern in the Carpet*, p. 13n.
14. See my *T. S. Eliot: Moments and Patterns*, p. 107.
15. Benson, *FitzGerald*, p. 66.
16. Joseph Conrad, *Youth* (Garden City: Doubleday, Page, 1923), pp. 36–37.
17. *Moments and Patterns*, p. 153.
18. *Selected Essays*, p. 4.

Chapter X

1. Mildred Martin, *A Half-Century of Eliot Criticism* (Lewisburg: Bucknell University Press, 1972).
2. *Poems in the Making* (Southhampton: University of Southampton, 1972), pp. 17, 29.
3. *The Sewanee Review*, 75 (1967), pp. 268–81.
4. See Warren's essay (especially the opening paragraph) "Continuity in T. S. Eliot's Literary Criticism," *The Sewanee Review*, 74 (1967), p. 272.
5. Beringause, "Journey through *The Waste Land*," pp. 79–80.
6. "John Ford," *Selected Essays*, p. 179.
7. *The Letters of Ezra Pound*, ed. D. D. Paige (New York: Harcourt Brace, 1950), pp. 169–71.
8. See above, Ch. V, n. 16.
9. Gardner, *Composition of Four Quartets*, pp. 160–61, 225.
10. Ibid., p. 67.
11. At earlier stages of this essay I had been vaguely tempted to see in Eliot's account of the "compound ghost," the "double part," and "another's voice" a remote and transmuted echo of Segismund's mirror ("the crystal on the wall"). There was a specific occasion which prepared me to yield to this temptation. I urged Professor James Wheatley to read the "Segismund" passage, expecting him to recognize the correspondences with "A Game of Chess." This he did, and he also just as confidently recognized the correspondence with the reflecting pool in *Burnt Norton* and the terza-rima lines in *Little Gidding*. His confident recognition soon produced for me a confidence of

recognition. It is a pleasure to acknowledge my indebtedness to Professor Wheatley and to express my gratitude for his having initiated this little case-history of stages and degrees of recognition.

12. The passages of verse quoted are Donne's *Satire III*, lines 79–82, and Quatrain 27 of FitzGerald's *Omar*. I regard FitzGerald's "About it and about" as an echoing of Donne's "about must and about must go," for the verbal similarity is enforced by contexts which are ultimately conceptual similarities.

There is ample evidence that FitzGerald read and admired Donne. In his own footnote to Quatrain 56 he wrote: "A curious mathematical Quatrain of Omar's has been pointed out to me; the more curious because almost exactly parallel'd by some verses of Doctor Donne's, that are quoted in Izaak Walton's Lives! Here is Omar: 'You and I are the image of a pair of compasses; though we have two heads (sc. our *feet*) we have one body; when we have fixed the centre for our circle, we bring our heads (sc. feet) together at the end.'" FitzGerald then proceeded to quote the last three stanzas of Donne's "A Valediction: Forbidding Mourning." Although Eliot does not quote these stanzas in his essay "The Metaphysical Poets," it is the first specific reference made to Donne's poetry in that essay: "the comparison of two lovers to a pair of compasses." The three stanzas in which the comparison is elaborated became a *locus classicus* of seventeenth-century metaphysical conceit in modern commentary on that subject.

A letter from FitzGerald to Edward Cowell (quoted by Benson, pp. 111–12), who first introduced FitzGerald to Persian, and to Omar, contains further evidence of the admiration for Donne. The letter is primarily about Omar: "I thought him from the first the most remarkable of the Persian Poets; and you keep finding out in him Evidences of logical Fancy which I had not dreamed of. I dare say these logical Riddles are not his best; but they are yet evidences of a Strength of mind which our Persian Friends rarely exhibit, I think. I always said about Cowley, Donne, etc., whom Johnson calls the metaphysical Poets, that their very Quibbles of Fancy showed a power of Logic which could follow Fancy through such remote Analogies. This is the case with Calderon's Conceits also." This emphasis on such merit as Johnson allowed the metaphysical poets prefigures Eliot's own revisions of Johnson's judgments and of the "Donne revival" generally. As for Calderón, there is only the passing reference, but I could not pass over it.

Appendix

La vida es sueño
(Acto segundo):

<table>
<tr><td>

(Salen músicos cantando,
y criados dando de vestir a Segismundo,
que sale como asombrado)

SEGISMUNDO
¡Válgame el cielo, qué veo!
¡Válgame el cielo, qué miro!
Con poco espanto lo admiro,
con mucha duda lo creo.
¿Yo en palacios suntuosos?
¿Yo entre telas y brocados?
¿Yo cercado de criados
tan lucidos y briosos?
¿Yo despertar de dormir
en lecho tan excelente?
¿Yo en medio de tanta gente
que me sirva de vestir?
Decir que es sueño es engaño;
bien sé que despierto estoy.
¿Yo Segismundo no soy?
Dadme, cielos, desengaño.
Decidme, ¿qué pudo ser
esto que a mi fantasía
sucedió mientras dormía,
que aquí me he llegado a ver?
Pero sea lo que fuere,
¿quién me mete en discurrir?
Dejarme quiero servir,
y venga lo que viniere.

</td><td>

(Enter musicians singing,
and servants clothing Segismund,
who seems amazed)

SEGISMUND
Good Heavens, what do I see!
Good heavens, what do I behold!
I marvel at it, but with slight alarm—
believe it, yet with much doubt.
I, in sumptuous palaces?
I, among fabrics and brocades?
I, surrounded by servants
so splendid and so eager?
I, waking from sleep
in such an elegant bed?
I, among so many people
who are helping me dress?
It's wrong to say this is a dream;
I know quite well I'm awake.
Am I not Segismund, I?
Heaven, reassure me.
Tell me—what could it be
that's happened to my imagination
while I was sleeping
that I find myself here?
But let that be as it may,
for who cares what I imagine?
I'll let myself be served,
and what comes of it may come.

</td></tr>
</table>

Pedro Calderón de la Barca, Tragedies (1),
ed. F. Ruiz Ramón (Madrid: Alianza
Editorial, 1967), pp. 80–81.

(My translation.
L. U.)

Index